VISITOR'S GUIDE

D1277685

Musical Instruments Museum

VISITOR'S GUIDE

MARDAGA

© Pierre Mardaga, éditeur and MIM
Hayen, 11 - B-4140 Sprimont (Belgique)
D. 2000-0024-11
I.S.B.N. 2-87009-730-1

Sommaire

Scientific direction
Malou Haine, Curator - Head of Department

Texts
Folk instruments in Belgium
Hubert Boone
European Folk instruments
Wim Bosmans
Instruments from outside Europe
Ignace De Keyser and Gretel Dumont
Western Art Music
Karel Moens, Mia Awouters, Ignace De Keyser, Pascale Vandervellen and
Anne Meurant
Strings and keyboards
Pascale Vandervellen, Mia Awouters and Luc Lannoo
Musicus mechanicus
Luc Lannoo and Ignace De Keyser

Translations
Jane Still, JohnWhitelaw, Julius Stenzel and Allen James

Coordination
Wim Bosmans, Allen James, Karel Moens, Anja Van Lerberghe and
Saskia Willaert

Illustrations
Anne Meurant

An asterisk (*) after the name of an instrument indicates that there is an
illustration.

Introduction

Since 11 January 1992 the Musical Instruments Museum (now known as the 'MIM') has been part of the Royal Museums of Art and History as Department IV. By royal decree, the State has recognised the scientific character of its activities and provided it with two sections: firstly, the early music section and secondly, the section of modern music (19th and 20th centuries), and popular and traditional music.

But the original creation of the Brussels Musical Instruments Museum dates from 1 February 1877, when it was attached to the Brussels Royal Music Conservatory with the didactic purpose of showing early instruments to the students. At the end of the 19th century, the creation of an official musical instruments museum was not a unique initiative. About twenty public collections already existed at the time the Brussels museum appeared, notably in Vienna (1814), Linz (1839), Stuttgart (1849), Munich (1854), Nuremberg (1856), South Kensington (1857), Paris (1861), Cambridge (1867), and Edinburgh (1869).

At the very beginning of the Brussels Musical Instruments Museum's creation two collections of instruments were joined together. One belonged to the celebrated Belgian musicologist François-Joseph Fétis (1784-1871), was bought by the Belgian government in 1872 and put on deposit in the Conservatory where Fétis was the first director. The other was offered to King Leopold II in 1876 by the Rajah Sourindro Mohun Tagore (1840-1914) and comprises about a hundred Indian instruments.

Victor-Charles Mahillon, the first curator

With these two original collections, the MIM was already remarkably rich for its time. But its first curator, Victor-Charles Mahillon (1841-1924) was considerably to augment its collections, thus placing it among the finest in the world. At his death in 1924, the MIM counted some 3666 articles, among which 3177 were original musical instruments. A collector and maker of wind instruments and a noted acoustics expert, Mahillon performed his job with an enthusiasm, competence and dynamism that exceeded any of the expectations that his purely honorary title might have aroused. Thanks to his activity and connections, the museum rapidly gained international fame, not only for the quantitative importance of its collections but also for their diversity, and for the quality and rarity of the items brought together.

In addition, between 1880 and 1922 Mahillon described the collections of the museum in a monumental five-volume catalogue. The catalogue also includes the four versions of his *Essay on the methodical classification of all instruments, ancient and modern* that was to serve as the basis for the classifications of E.M. von Hornbostel and C. Sachs which are still used today. This classification of musical instruments entitled him to be considered as one of the pioneers of organology, the science of musical instruments.

Beginning in 1877, Mahillon created a restoration workshop in the MIM where he employed and trained a worker, Franz de Vestibule, to restore damaged articles, and also to make copies of instruments from other public collections of which no original examples existed in Brussels. In the 1880s historical concerts on early instruments or copies were organised by François-Auguste Gevaert, who succeeded Fétis at the head of the Brussels Royal Music Conservatory. Performed by Conservatory professors and students, these concerts were a great success in Brussels and London at the end of the 19th century.

Through astute judgment, Mahillon obtained large augmentations of the collections by calling on philanthropists, by mixing with erudite amateurs who sometimes became generous donors, and through friendly relations with Belgian diplomats in foreign posts such as Jules Van Aalst at Canton (China) and Dorenberg at Puebla (Mexico), who brought back several instruments from beyond Europe. It was thus that Mahillon received or purchased isolated pieces of great historical and organological value, but also homogeneous ensembles whose interest today is considerable. Mahillon followed all the large public sales of musical instruments and bought the pieces he needed to complete the ideal collection he was determined to build at the MIM. A very rare Chédeville bagpipe came from the Coussemaker collection (1877). From the Tolbecque collection (1879) Mahillon acquired 129 interesting pieces including the famous componium by the Dutchman Winkel, a mechanical instrument unique in the world. From the Adolphe Sax collection at Paris (1877), the MIM grew by thirty-seven instruments of diverse origins. In 1883 Mahillon sold to the MIM his own private collection of 369 instruments, the majority of which were wind instruments. In the 1890s the colonial Dumoutier donated seven Vietnamese instruments and sold about fifty others. Several crumhorns, shawms and *bajoncillos* come from the Barbieri collection (1902). Two collections, because of their remarkable contents, merit more detailed descriptions.

The Contarini-Correr collection

Bought in 1886, this collection consists of a group of 121 Italian and German instruments from the 16th and 17th centuries. It comprises a complete 17th century orchestra, including two viola da gamba families built by Pietro Zenatto in 1683 and 1684. Also present are several harpsichords and organs, of which one was made in 1676 in Piazzola by the German maker Theodor Agathe. These instruments were brought together during the 17th century by Prince Marco Contarini (1631-1689), proctor of San Marco in Venice. In his villa at Piazzola sub Brenta in the province of Padua, this patron of the arts maintained a music-school where girls learned to sing and play all sorts of instruments, stringed, keyboard and wind. These schools were quite extensive in Italy; as we all know, Vivaldi taught at a similar school in Venice, the *Conservatorio dell'Ospedale della Pietà*. This collection must have been quite famous at the time, as Jacques Chassebras de Cramailles described it in the *Mercure galant* of February 1681.

Through inheritance, the Contarini collection passed to the Correr family. In 1869 the French collector Fau was able to examine the collection and acquire a dozen instruments which he then offered to the Paris Musical Instruments Museum. In 1872 a few instruments were bought by an English collector and later acquired by the London Royal College of Music. But the rest of the collection joined the MIM. Long considered to be rigourously authentic instruments, a few are nevertheless being challenged today by modern scientific techniques.

The Snoeck collection

The Renaix lawyer and collector César Snoeck (1832-1898) built a major collection of some 2,000 instruments. This collection was dispersed at his death. A first part including some 1,200 instruments was acquired by the Emperor Wilhelm II and offered to the *Hochschule für Musik* in Berlin. Unfortunately, most of these instruments were destroyed during the Second World War. A second lot of 363 pieces was bought by Baron Stackelberg, director of the imperial chapel of St Petersburg, for the estate of Tsar Nicholas II. These instruments are still part of the St Petersburg Instrument Museum. In 1899 there still remained for sale a part of the collection comprising the instruments of the Low Countries, including 437 pieces.

Less interested by the preceding lots which included many articles he already had, Mahillon nevertheless hoped that the lot of instruments from our own regions would not go abroad, the more so since at the time the MIM contained barely a hundred. He mentioned it to Louis Cavens (1850-1940), an enlightened philanthropist of major Belgian scientific institutions, who bought the collection with his own money and immediately offered it to the Museum.

Bowed stringed instruments constitute the most interesting part of the collection, for the variety of instruments represented as well as for the different schools of makers. There are many violins, violas, violoncellos, double-basses, kit-violins, treble viols, violas d'amore, violas da gamba and guitars, offering a representative panorama of the work of dozens of makers from Antwerp, Brussels, Ghent and Liège from the 17th to the 19th centuries. Although less numerous, harpsichord-type instruments are particularly appreciated, as the Ruckers dynasty of Antwerp is represented by seven instruments, notably a 1619 spinet-harpsichord of which only one other example exists in the world. A spinet by the Tournai maker Delin, two anonymous fretted clavichords, a Bible organ and a positive organ are also among the jewels of this collection. Wind instruments, however, are the most numerous: 198 pieces, including clarinets, oboes, bassoons, contrabassoons, flutes, flageolets, fifes and serpents, illustrate the work of the Rottenburghs at Brussels, the Tuerlinckx family at Mechelen, Carré and Dupré at Tournai, and Raingo at Mons. As for the brass instruments, they date principally from the 19th century and include new inventions of the period: ophicleides, keyed trumpets and horns, omnitonic horns, piston instruments and tubas and trombones from the workshops of Mahillon, Moeremans, De Backer, Van Belle, and many others. Finally, we should note that the Snoeck collection includes several popular instruments such as Jew's harps, *rommelpots*, bagpipes, Vosges spinets, etc. Because of its variety and quality, the collection is exceptionally interesting.

The collections after Mahillon

The growth of the collection slowed sharply after Mahillon's death in 1924. His successor, Ernest Closson (1870-1950), was nonetheless motivated by the same scientific curiosity regarding musical instruments. He edited several articles on Belgian makers for the *National Biography* and devoted a long monograph to *La facture des instruments de musique en Belgique* which appeared on the occasion of the Universal Exhibition held at Brussels in 1935. Besides organological information, statistics show the volume of Belgian instrument exports in the mid-19th century and highlight (alas!) the reversal of trends in the 1920s and 1930s, namely the disappearance of most of the instrument builders in our regions.

After the First World War, donors and philanthropists became rarer. From 1924 to 1968, only about a thousand instruments entered the collections. Until 1957, the curators taking their turn at the head of the MIM, Ernest Closson (from 1924 to 1936), his son Herman (from 1936 to 1945) and René Lyr (from 1945 to 1957), had little choice but to limit themselves to preserving the assembled instruments, in not always satisfactory conditions, the budget allotted to the Museum being totally insufficient.

With the arrival of Roger Bragard (1903-1985), curator from 1957 to 1968, the situation improved considerably. This eminent Latinist, drawn to musicology by his persistent interest for ancient treatises relating to music, was able to attract the attention of the Minister of Culture at the time and particularly of Miss Sara Huysmans: budgets were considerably augmented, the exhibition rooms were renovated, guides and scientific personnel were hired, and concerts of early music on original instruments or copies were organised. Once again rare pieces could be acquired for the collections. Bragard's efforts were continued by René de Maeyer (from 1968 to 1989), who hired about ten scientific collaborators, each specialised in a different field of organology. Nicolas Meeùs assumed the interim from 1989 to 1994: he launched the project for moving to Old England. Under the present director, Malou Haine, this project has been realised, along with the development of several projects.

Current acquisitions policy is diverse. It aims not only to seek pieces illustrating the variety of work by makers in Western Europe and, more particularly, our own regions and France, but also instruments whose complex actions are not yet represented in the collections. A particular effort is made to acquire instruments representative of modern times. Finally, the MIM also tries to buy old instruments in playing order so that they can be heard in concerts.

The installation of the MIM in Old England, rue Montagne de la Cour

Shortly after the creation of the Museum in 1877, the collections were stocked in the rue aux Laines, in an annexe of the Royal Music Conservatory, which had been housed in a new building designed by the architect Jean-Pierre Cluysenaar. The Conservatory, in the rue de la Régence, also received a bourgeois house on the corner of the Petit Sablon into which moved the director, François-Auguste Gevaert (1828-1908). With the growth of the collection, it became necessary to find more room and to have better conditions for the reserves. The situation became critical to the point that an important donor, Louis Cavens, threatened to withdraw the instruments that he had given to the MIM if the government did not take adequate action. A promise was made to him, but only a temporary solution was found. The reserves in the rue aux Laines were enlarged and the beautiful building on the corner of the Sablon was transformed into exhibition rooms.

It was only at the end of the 1970s that the federal state was led to realise the necesssity of finding a global solution for the MIM, then dispersed in about fifteen buildings near the Sablon and in the north of Brussels. The former Old England was bought in 1978, to be completely redeveloped to house the exhibition rooms, the reserve and the administration of the MIM. This building had two very stylistically disparate elements. The neo-classic building on the corner of the Place Royale was part of the global conception of the square by the architect Barnabé Guimard, who took his inspiration from the Place Stanislas in Nancy. As for the building in the rue Montagne de la Cour, it is one of the most beautiful art nouveau buildings in Brussels. It dates from 1899 and was designed by the architect Paul Saintenoy. The decision was made to add a third building in the rue Villa Hermosa to house the instrument reserve. The interior was transformed to bring it up to modern standards of security. Air conditioning ensures optimal conservation of the instruments. Studies and the actual work took several years. The MIM officially received the keys of the building in December 1998. The transfer of the collections took place in 1999 and required ten months of moving. The new MIM opened in June 2000.

New activities

With the installation of the MIM in this new location also came the aim of setting up new activities. The MIM may have turned inwards in studying its own collections in the past, but it has now resolved to play a role in the city and to open itself up to a larger public.

Any museum must answer three fundamental questions: preservation and conservation of its patrimony and making it available to the public. The first two questions are the task of restorers and technicians, who work in collaboration with those responsible for the collections. The third question especially concerns publications and specific activities for visitors: exhibitions, educational visits and cultural activities. The exhibition area has been arranged into an attractive path divided into ninety-odd themes over the four floors of the exhibition area. Each floor is centred on a particular section: the ground floor (0) shows popular instruments, from Belgium and Europe as well as extra-European instruments; the first floor (+1) gives an historical tour, from antiquity to the 20th century; the second floor (+2) is presented more systematically, showing the development of keyboard instruments and stringed instruments. The basement (-1) shows the mechanical instruments, 20th century instruments and bells. In all, about 1,500 instruments are shown and more than 700 documents add to the information given on the information boards.

1. The Musical Instruments Museum (MIM). On the left is the Saintenoy building housing the reception; on the right the Guimard building with four levels of exhibition area, the concert hall and the administration. MIM, Brussels; photo Jean Boucher

It would be sad to see the instruments without hearing them. The different themes of the exhibitions are illustrated by listening to works related to the instruments on display. By means of infra-red headphones, the visitor can listen to about two hundred musical extracts, from ancient Greece to the music of Varèse of the middle of the 20th century. The MIM has made a special effort for musical activities for children: special workshops have been set up for young children and adolescents. A Garden of Orpheus has been made in the basement (-1): this playing area allows children to discover musical instruments in a magic and enchanting environment. Many guided tours are organised for schools and other groups. Finally a Sound Space has been opened in the basement level (-1) to show how sound is produced by different types of musical instrument.

In addition, the MIM has re-established its former policy of giving concerts. Many Brussels citizens will still remember the concerts given in period costume in the 1960s in the Petit Sablon, as well as the concerts of Renaissance and Baroque music that were given in the Grand Sablon some twenty years later. Now, a 200 place concert hall, on the 5th floor of the Guimard building, allows the organisation of regular concerts. These are not only of old music, but include popular music and music from all over the world. The aim is to highlight the value of the collections. Several keyboard

2. The interior of the Saintenoy building. MIM, Brussels; photo Jean Boucher

instruments, such as harpsichords, virginals, square pianos and grand pianos of the collection are regularly played at MIM concerts. The MIM has just launched a series of recordings of the instruments of the collections.

Soon there will open temporary exhibitions to illustrate less well-known aspects of the collections or to show instruments from other public or private collections. It should be noted that the library, specialised in works on musical instruments and musical iconography, remains, as previously, at the disposition of students, researchers and instrument makers. To end the visit, the public can go up to the restaurant or tea room on the 6th floor, where there is a panoramic view of Brussels.

Efforts by public bodies

Along with the considerable investment allowed by the *Régie des Bâtiments* for the renovation and fitting out of Old England, the *Ministre de la Politique scientifique* wished to allocate appropriate means to the MIM for its functioning. Special funds were released to pay for the decoration of the rooms. In addition, the personnel has increased considerably, from about twenty in 1995 to more than seventy in 2000. Several people who are concerned with pedagogical and cultural activities have joined the team of scientists. The administrative personnel has been increased, and technicians (engineers, computer scientists and electricians) now bring their competences to the different services of the MIM. The security and reception personnel are all new. Our administration, the S.S.T.C. (*Services scientifiques, techniques et culturels*), have played a determining role in these developments by their confidence in us and their constant help.

The sponsors

Despite the important financial investment by public bodies, it came clear that it would be necessary to appeal to sponsors, both private and public, to realise certain projects not covered by public funding. The complete list of our benefactors and the projects they have supported is on the last page of this *Visitor's Guide*. Some sponsors have even decided to maintain their financial contribution after the opening of the MIM to encourage recurrent activities. Our greatest thanks go to the public bodies and the sponsors. Without them, the MIM would not have been able to open its doors under such favourable conditions.

Malou Haine

Head of department
Curator of the MIM

FOLK INSTRUMENTS
IN BELGIUM

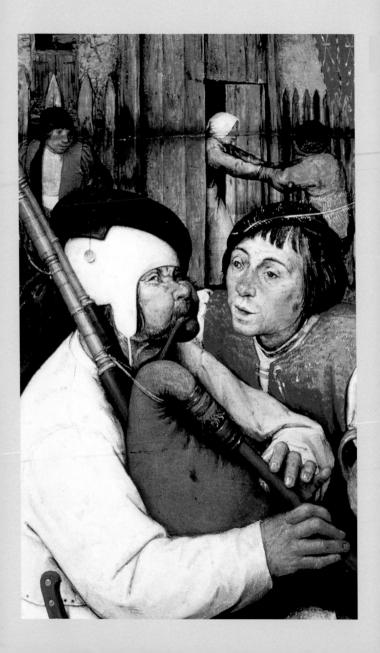

A word of introduction

This exhibition gives a general view of the Belgian patrimony of folk instruments. The most important families of instrument are presented by type, while the others are associated with a particular theme, such as the instruments of the calendar.

The folk instruments of this country are part of the musical culture of Western Europe. Their dissemination was little influenced by the presence of national or linguistic frontiers. Thus, the bagpipe of the north of Hainaut is closely related to the types of bagpipes found in the centre of France. Between our plucked dulcimer and those of the Vosges, there are few organological differences. Our oldest hurdy-gurdies often resemble those of Germany and Central Europe. The most archaic instruments naturally show even greater uniformity: the bark and earthenware whistles, bark horns and Jew's harps have the same form all over Europe.

However, there are a few noteworthy regional characteristics. The *rommelpot* is known only in Flanders, although it is virtually indistinguishable from the friction drums of the south of France and the Iberian peninsula. It should be noted that the Flemish and Walloon instrumental patrimonies are particularly rich when they are compared to those of many other European countries. Thanks to its very easy access, this region has always been open to outside influences. Flemish and Walloons have constantly enriched their musical culture with the best innovations of their neighbours. This assimilation of foreign elements has almost always been carried out with discernment.

The revival of folk music since the sixties

During the 1960s, different regions of Europe started to become interested in their own musical traditions. It was above all in the Anglo-Saxon countries, as well as countries with a Celtic heritage, that this new tendency found an echo. Our regions, however, were also in the vanguard. Thus, from 1962 on, Rose Thisse-Derouette noted and published Walloon dance tunes in a series of booklets. In 1964 the *Vlaams Dansarchief* (Archive of Flemish Dances) was founded in Schoten, near to Antwerp. In the same year, the Antwerp singer Wannes Van de Velde started a programme of popular Flemish songs, followed by a first recording in 1966. Until then, interest was focused on dances and popular songs.

Yet, little by little, the interest in instrumental folk music gained ground. The group *De Vlier* started in 1968 in Nederokkerzeel in Flemish Brabant. This folk group soon put out a record of regional dances played on old instruments like the single action accordion, the bagpipe and the plucked dulcimer. A few months later saw the start of the group *'t Kliekske*, an ensemble which did much pioneering work. They were followed by groups like *Jan Smed*, *De Kadullen* and *De Speelmannen*. This revival was also known in Wallonia, with groups like *Les Pêleteûs*, *Les Zûnants Plankèts* and *Rue du Village*. In the 1980s, even if the fashion for folk music had faded, interest in this art was maintained. In the meantime, we have seen the opening of a series of centres which organise specialised courses. The most important are those of

Neufchâteau (since 1975), Borzée and Gooik. As for amateur makers, they are well served by the courses at the *Volksmuziekstages* at Gooik as well as at the *Centrum voor muziekinstrumentenbouw* (CMB) of Puurs.

1. The plucked dulcimer: an instrument for playing at home

The plucked dulcimer tradition in our regions goes back to the 17th century, as shown by an instrument from Boezinge near Ypres. It was destroyed in the First World War, but the MIM has an exact copy, built earlier. Years before, this plucked dulcimer was used for accompanying sacred songs in the local church. As for the others, only a few 18th and 19th century Belgian examples have survived. The golden age of the plucked dulcimer began after 1900 and peaked between 1918 and 1935. At that time it was a favoured domestic instrument often played by women. The folk music revival of the 1970s saw the plucked dulcimer reappear, notably in folk bands.

Belgian models usually have a trapezoidal or rectangular case. Many examples have double cases, a second sound box added below the first. This construction technique was mainly practiced in the Meuse valley near Dinant and Andenne, and in West Flanders. The finest examples often come from the latter province, although the oldest have been found in the Hageland and south Kempen.

The plucked dulcimer is equipped with a range of metallic frets over which pass three to six melodic strings tuned in unison. Most often there are also three or four drones, tuned either in unison or in a chord. Certain Brabant or Kempen models have twelve drones (3 x 4) producing three different chords, G, C and D, for example. All the strings are

3. Plucked dulcimer, Kortrijk, c. 1905 (inv. HB198)

Double sound box, reddish-coloured, in elm and beech. Four melodic strings and three drones. This typical example of careful West Flanders construction was played by Leontina Dekant (1904-1987) of Zwevegem.

4. Bertha Cleynhens (1902-1983). Hever, Flemish Brabant, 1976. MIM, Brussels; photo Geert Vermeiren

This Brabant peasant normally played within her family circle. Her repertoire included a few traditional melodies, dances in fashion before the Second World War like the waltz and schottische, and a few contemporary favourites.

metallic and are plucked with a plectrum. The melodic strings are pushed against the chosen fret with a stick. Most instruments have a diatonic scale with an extra semitone between the 7th and 8th degree, and a range of a little more than two octaves.

In Dutch, the term *hommel* is used only in scientific contexts. Flemish folk terms are *epinet, spinet, blokviool, klompviool, vlier* and *krabkas*, whereas in Wallonia they are *bûche de Meuse, épinette* and *épinette des bateliers*.

2. The dulcimer: a folk instrument for the bourgeois

Probably it was the Crusaders who first brought the dulcimer to the Low Countries in the 12th century. In fact, the Low Countries were an important pipeline for the instrument's eventual spread into the rest of Europe. In 15th century iconography, the dulcimer is most often shown in the hands of an angel; later documents tend to give it to women. Archives and various sources sporadically mention its use by travelling musicians. In the Low Countries, however, the dulcimer was much more widespread among the bourgeois. It disappeared from our traditions around the mid-19th century. The last known player was a Brussels street musician nicknamed *Jaekske met zijn hakkeberd* ('Jackie with his dulcimer'), still active around 1850.

The earliest iconography usually depicts an instrument consisting of a simple flat panel equipped with five to twelve strings passing over one or two bridges. The dulcimer evolved rapidly; by the beginning of the 16th century it had arrived at its finished form. The few surviving examples date from the 17th and 18th centuries. Their sound boxes are all trapezoidal and their construction elaborate. A few are inlaid, some attractively decorated with painted flowers or foliage. The range of these instruments covers twenty-five to thirty notes, with three or four strings for each course. The courses are divided in order to obtain three registers, one bass (to the right of the bass bridge) and two melodic (separated by the interval of a fifth) on either side of the treble bridge. The dulcimer is played with two fine, flexible hammers, curved at the forward end and covered with felt or some other soft material. The Flemish term *hakkebord* is in fact the name of a chopping-board, a kitchen utensil used to cut up finely meat and vegetables. French speaking regions use the term *tympanon*. However, in an old series of bilingual dictionaries *hakkebord* was often translated as *psalterion*, a term that should rather apply to another related instrument, but with plucked strings.

5. Dulcimer, Flanders, 17th or 18th century (inv. M2946)
Trapezoidal sound box with pine sound board, edges gilt-threaded and ornamented with dark green foliage. Two bell shaped flowers in each of the two anterior corners. Two gilded pasteboard roses. Ribs apparently of apple, painted black as are the bridges. The instrument has seventeen strings in four courses, originally there were probably eighteen.

3. The hurdy-gurdy: an instrument played by beggars and the blind

Already in the 13th century the Flemish author Jacob van Maerlant mentioned the hurdy-gurdy in his *Trojaensche Oorlog*. A little later it was again mentioned in the *Geste de Liège* by the chronicler Jehan des Preis (Jean d'Outremeuse), and in the *Livre des Mestiers*, a bilingual Bruges manual. The first representations of the instrument also date from this period, but it was principally between the 16th and 18th centuries that the hurdy-gurdy took its place in folk music. After a few sporadic manifestations until the mid-19th century it disappeared from the popular milieu. Towards 1970 the hurdy-gurdy began to attract attention again and today there are dozens of players.

6. Hurdy-gurdy, Flanders, probably 18th century (inv. M2904)

Body in the shape of a violoncello, walnut ribs, pine back and sound board. The key-box, peg-box and certain other parts are painted in black. This hurdy-gurdy, one of the rare surviving Belgian examples, has a chromatic keyboard of thirty keys (two series of fifteen), two melodic strings and two drones, but no trompette.

The instrument consists of a sound box on which is fixed a rectangular key-box. It contains one or two sets of keys that slide from back to front; placed at a right angle to their end are tangents that shorten the melodic string. After having been touched and released, the key automatically returns to its initial position, due to the instrument's oblique playing position and helped by the string's vibration. Most of the hurdy-gurdies from the Low Countries have one or two melodic strings and two to four drones. Instruments equipped with a *trompette* (trumpet bridge), a string used to mark the rhythm, are rather rare, though more commonly found in France. The strings are bowed by a flat-edged wheel turned by a crank. In the past the instrument was often used by blind beggars.

7. Jan van de Venne (1616-1651), *Musician beggars.* © Kunsthistorisches Museum Wien

Period iconography indicates that local hurdy-gurdies were rarely equipped with a trompette. Because of this, many players were accompanied by a small boy playing a triangle to mark the rhythm.

Early Flemish terms are *symphonie, lier, boerenlier* (peasant's lyre) and *blindenlier* (blindman's lyre) but the term *draailier* (turning-lyre) has long taken precedence. In Wallonia, the French term *vielle à roue* is used, with regional variations like *vierlète* and *tiesse di tch'va* (horse's head), a term which probably refers to the form of the sound-box.

4. The accordion or the poor man's piano

The first Belgian accordion workshop was created in Brussels a little before 1840 by François Verhasselt. It remained active until 1853. Its instruments have a diatonic melodic keyboard and, most often, two chord keys. These early models are diatonic or single action: each key produces two different notes, one when the bellows are pulled and the other when they are pushed. After 1870 the Solari and Scheerlinck shops* opened in the capital. Their instruments, also single action, had two or three series of keys and six to twelve chord buttons.

Towards 1880, the Callewaert family created the first Flemish workshop, first at Zwevezele and later at Lichtervelde. It was a great success. The period between 1900 and 1925 saw the appearance of other workshops like those of Van Houtte, Decap, Van Roten, Meulemans and Schram.

8. Single action accordion, Vital Scheerlinck, Brussels, c. 1900 (inv. HB188)

Rectangular sound-box with moulding in *doucine*, veneer in Brazilian rosewood and brass framings. Melodic keyboard with three rows of keys; bass keyboard with ten spoon-keys (2 x 5) and two buttons. The bellows assembly has eleven folds and is decorated with peacock-tail paper.

9. Edmond Croibien (1910-1997), Ciney, Namur, 1980. MIM, Brussels; photo Christian De Bruyne

The musician is playing a double action accordion with a Namur keyboard from Vassart-Lefèvre of Auvelais, and a foot-bass by the Namur maker Marchal. Croibien was the last Walloon musician of the older generation to use the foot-bass.

At Auvelais, near Namur, Vassart inaugurated the first Walloon workshop in 1884. The province of Namur became an important accordion making centre, with Alexandry, Coppée, Marchal and Limage, amongst others. The instruments, now chromatic or double action*, were equipped with three rows of keys on each side, each producing one note. There were therefore no preset chords. From the First World War onwards, accordions with preset chords were made in the Liège ateliers of Léva-Giboreau and Gris. The last shops were those of Sabatini in Charleroi and Boland in Waregem, making modern instruments. Fierce competition from abroad ended this rich Belgian building tradition in 1957.

In most regions, the instrument is called accordion or harmonica. There also exist many regional Flemish denominations like *trekzak* (pull-bag), *tienbasser* (ten-basser), *pierelare* and *open-en-toe* (open-and-shut). For Namur, note the old term *bour-èt-satche* or *satche-èt-r-boute*, composed of *bourer* (to push) and *satchî* (to pull).

A variant on the accordion is the 'foot-bass' (in French, *basse-aux pieds* or *basse pédale*, in Flemish, *voetbas*). This is a trapezoidal box with a bellows and, most often, twelve keys on the upper surface. The foot-bass works only by expulsion of air: when a key is pressed, the bellows closes simultaneously. The instrument produces only fundamental bass-notes and was used principally to accompany Namur accordions. It was invented by the Namur maker Alexandry in 1894.

5. Flutes: a rich diversity

There are a surprising number of different types of flute in our musical heritage. One of the oldest is the tabor pipe: a duct flute, much like a recorder but with only two finger holes and one thumb hole. This flute can be seen in illustrations from as early as the end of the 13th century and remained in fashion until about the middle of the 17th century. Players of the tabor pipe, usually minstrels, jesters and jugglers, would accompany themselves on a drum called a tabor.

The fife* is a small keyless transverse flute, which was probably introduced into the Low Countries by Swiss mercenaries at the end of the 15th century. This instrument still plays an important role in Belgian folklore, especially in the region between the Sambre and the Meuse. In many villages religious processions are escorted by pseudo-military bands in (post-)Napoleonic-style uniforms, playing fifes and drums. Important centres of this tradition are Gerpinnes, Walcourt and Thuin. The musical repertoire is made up largely of marches and signals. The fife playing tradition has also survived in the south of East Flanders. Nowadays the instrument is once again becoming a part of many folk bands.

The history of the six-hole duct flute also goes back to the Middle Ages. These flutes were originally made of wood or bone; some began to have keys from the 19th century onwards. By the middle of the 19th century cheap tin whistles made in England and Germany flooded into the market.

The ocarina is usually made of terracotta. It was introduced into Belgium in 1876 and was a great success. Around 1900 ocarina orchestras made up of different sized ocarinas could be found in various places. However, this golden age lasted only for a very short time.

10. Fifes and drums of the Thuin Second Imperial Infantry Regiment of Sappers and Grenadiers, Gerpinnes, 1986. © Le Soir; photo J. Heylemans

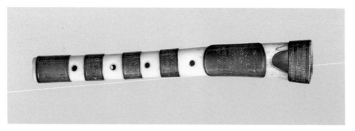

11. Flageolet (duct flute), copy of an instrument of 1608 of the Guild of Saint Sebastian of Lokeren, East Flanders (inv. M1042)

Copy of an instrument given in 1608 to the Guild of Saint Sebastian by the Archduke and Archduchess Albert and Isabelle. It is made of a sheep femur, decorated with six silver rings on which are engraved the names of the members of the guild. This flute has four finger holes, two thumb holes and a flattened mouthpiece with a wooden stop.

Various other instruments belong to the family of duct flutes such as the flageolet*, which has four finger holes, two thumb holes and sometimes also a number of keys. It was in use between the 17th and 19th centuries and was particularly popular amongst the middle classes. There was also a double flageolet and a 'horn' flute — made from a cow's horn, where the player's lip served as a stop. As for the bark whistle, carved from a small willow or ash branch, this too belongs to the family of duct flutes, primitive though it may be.

6. The drums: the heartbeat of the procession

Different types of drum can be found in Belgium. The tabor and the tambourine, which are seen in representations from as early as the end of the 13th century, are in fact the oldest types of drum. The player of the tabor would play a tabor pipe at the same time. This drum was usually small and would have a membrane on each side. The tambourine, however, has only one membrane and usually has jingles or small bells attached. In Flanders it is called a *schellentrom* or a *rinkelbom* (jingle drum). In West Flanders they use the strange term of *boerhavezeven*; this refers to the (half-)sieve used by the peasants to sieve flour. The French terms are *tambourin* and *tambour de basque*.

The best known type of drum is the side drum*, popular from the end of the 15th century. It was originally a military instrument that was quickly adopted by the guilds of archers and other associations. Up until the 18th century the barrel, or body, was made of a thin piece of curved wood, this later changed to a sheet of brass. Very often it would be decorated with painted heraldic motifs. The side drum always has two membranes stretched by hoops and a zigzag rope. The snare, a double thread of catgut, passes over the lower head and it is the vibration of this snare that gives the particular penetrating sound.

12a. Side drum, Flanders, 1763 (inv. M2552A)

Brass barrel decorated with a motif in relief: shield, initials 'HMQF', dated 1763. This drum has a double snare.

12b. Lansquenet drum, Flanders, end of the 18th or beginning of the 19th century (inv. M2553)

Barrel made of four stacked cylinders in beech, decorated with heraldic motifs: a red lion with a stylised lily in a white crown on his front.

13. The famous drummers of Binche, and several *Gilles* during the Carnival festivities, before 1940. © IRPA, Brussels

In Binche and the surrounding areas, the bass drum is carried on the back of the person in front of the player.

This type of drum is always played with two drumsticks.

The lansquenet drum* has a deeper barrel or body than the side drum (usually from 65 to 70cm). It is made of a series of two to four wooden cylinders, one on top of the other. It does not usually have a snare and is played with two felted drum sticks.

In conclusion, we should mention the small side drum and the bass drum, which first appeared at the beginning of the 19th century. Nowadays the side drum and small side drum play an important part in musical tradition, particularly around Binche* and between the Sambre and the Meuse.

7. The fiddle: an instrument of minstrels

Already in the 13th century, sources in Northwestern Europe speak of bowed stringed instruments which can be seen as forerunners of the violin. In the early 16th century, iconographic documents show instruments which resemble the classical violin, both by their shape and by their construction. From the 17th century, we see the fiddle being played at village fairs and weddings, often with the bagpipe, the hurdy-gurdy, or the transverse flute. Later there is the duo fiddle-bass viol (later to be replaced by a large violoncello) which subsisted in some regions up to and even after the First World War. Many groups like the guilds of archers would hire the services of a fiddler who could play fashionable dances as well as their own traditional repertoire.

14. Henri Schmitz (1904-1977), Champs (Bertogne), Luxemburg, 1972.
Photo Rémy Dubois

This slate-worker of the Ardennes learned the fiddle from a very young age, as well as the clarinet and the accordion. He was one of the last village fiddlers in Belgium, and he played an important part in the revival of Walloon folk music in the 1970s. There are several extant recordings of his playing.

Village fiddlers* usually played their dance tunes in the keys of D, G and A. Their basic technique consisted of short, snappy, detached bow strokes often accompanied by striking the lower open string. Some players held the bow not at the frog, but closer to the centre; others placed the little finger of the bow hand not above, but below the screw. They played without vibrato and rarely left the first position.

We have the notebooks of 18th and 19th century fiddlers, of which the most well-known are those of Walloon musicians such as Wandenbrile of Namur, Lambert of Champlon, Jamin of Meix-devant-Virton and Houssa of Soy. Both their repertoire and their style resemble, sometimes very closely, that of the dancing-master violinists who worked among the bourgeoisie.

In the 19th century, with the arrival of wind instruments into popular orchestras, the violin took a back seat. But the old violin keys were long used in mixed ensembles of winds and strings; thus clarinets and cornets were made in A, flutes and trombones in C. This tradition disappeared after the First World War, but lately, some groups are playing again in this old tradition.

8. The bagpipe: instrument of shepherds and dancers

Beginning in the 13th century, written sources such as the *Cleomadès* of Adenet le roi spoke of the bagpipe in the Southern Low Countries, whereas the first iconographical evidence dates only from about 1320. We see it first in pastoral scenes, but from the 15th century, it was shown being used in secular festivities. Thus among the seventy-one musicians accompanying the famous *Ommegang* pageant in Dendermonde in 1477, there are no fewer than twenty-eight bagpipe players. The high point of the bagpipe came a century later, when it was impossible to imagine fairs and wedding celebrations without it. In the 18th century it began to give way to the fiddle-bass duo, and less than a century later, it sat on the sidelines. Only in the north of the Hainaut region did any significant tradition survive, and that until about 1885. Until the First World War, there were occasional players to be found, but then the instrument virtually disappeared until the mid 1950s, when the Brussels painter Jacques Laudy built his first reconstructions. From the 1970s, a revival took place, and we can now find more than two hundred bagpipe players spread across Belgium.

We have had here many different types of bagpipes in the past, but for centuries two types have predominated. The first, found mostly in Flanders, has two parallel drone pipes*. The second, spread across the Hainaut area, has a small drone placed parallel to the chanter, with the large drone carried on the shoulder. In both cases, the player keeps the bag filled with air by blowing into a blowpipe. The chanter has a conical bore with a double reed;

15. Pieter Bruegel the Elder (c. 1525-1569), *Peasants' Dance* **(detail).**
© Kunsthistorisches Museum Wien

the drones are cylindrical with a single reed. Only three examples of the Hainaut-type instrument have been preserved; all are in the MIM collection. Old Flemish words for the bagpipe are *quene*, *ruispijp*, *moezel* and *zakpijp*. In the 18th century the terms *moezelzak* and *doedelzak* came into use. In the Liège area, we find the terms *pipsac* and *panse*, the Picard dialect of the Hainaut speaks of *muchosa*, *muchafou* and *cornefou* — the Latin *follis* (bag) being deformed into *fou*. Around Eupen, one speaks of *Düdelsack* and *Pitschbüel* (squeeze-bag), and in Arlon it is a *Trutelsack*.

16. Bagpipe, Arc-Ainières, Hainaut, late 18th or first half of the 19th century (inv. M2702)

The instrument is made of the following parts: goatskin bag (renewed), blowpipe, chanter, two drones and three stocks connected to the reservoir. The pipes are turned from different kinds of wood, the horn is reinforced by a ring of animal horn and brass. It was played by Thomas Piron (1824-1892) of Arc-Ainières (Frasnes-lez-Anvaing).

9. The Jew's harp: you can buy it at the fair

Written sources testify to the presence of the Jew's harp in the Low Countries already in the 14th century. It is mentioned in a Flemish erotic song in the *Gruuthuse* MS in Bruges (c. 1380-1390) as well as in a petition dated 1397 in Hainaut. A little later, a student of Memling painted a Jew's harp in the hands of an angel. Its golden age was the 16th and 17th centuries; in the 18th century it was treated as a child's toy and fell into disuse. It was probably rediscovered in the 19th century. Around 1835, the Jew's harp even entered bourgeois society with the influence of Joseph Mattau, a Brussels dancing-master. Subsequently, the tradition declined, completely disappearing in the period between the two world wars. In about 1970, the last remaining players could give but little information, but there is now some new interest.

17. Jew's harp, Oudenaarde, 16th century? (inv. M2549/1)

Cast iron body. The tongue is set in a double flanged slot. It is richly ornamented with engraved motifs: leaves, flowers and arabesques, etc. The frame carries the following inscription: 'Ivstinvs Lievax Avdenaerde / Vast int hand ver van tand' ('Firmly in the hand, far from the teeth').

18. Engraving by Jan Wierix after Pieter Bruegel the Elder (c. 1525-1569), *Every merchant praises his wares.* © KBR, Brussels, SI 7737 VB.175-L.69

In various pictorial documents from the 16th and 17th centuries, the Jew's harp is seen being sold by peddlars who normally are also selling flutes, nets, and eyeglasses. The caption of this engraving proclaims, 'Here you have nets and Jew's harps, as well as lovely flutes; better wares are not to be found'.

Our instruments are made from brass, iron or bronze, sometimes moulded. The vibrating tongue is attached to the body in different ways. The end of the tongue is folded at a 90° angle and finishes in a loop. The instrument is placed in the mouth with the two arms of the frame against the teeth in such a way that the tongue can freely vibrate inside the mouth cavity. Normally one plucks the tongue with the right-hand index finger. The instrument only produces overtones, which form melodies by changing the size and shape of the mouth cavity.

The old Flemish terms for the instrument are *tromp* and *boerentromp* (peasant trumpet), but the terms *mondtrom* and *mondharp* (mouth harp) have long been in use. In Wallonia, it was formerly called the *gawe*, from the French *joue* and the English 'jaw', going back to the Latin *gauta*. It was called *trompe* in the Picardy dialect, but the current universally-used French term is *guimbarde*.

10. Calendar instruments

The use of certain instruments and natural sound producers are specific to precise seasons of the year. Thus, the bark horn and the bark and pottery whistles are connected to the springtime. The last-named are in fact duct flutes with a mouth-piece and a lip. There are innumerable models, usually made in the shape of a chicken or a pig. They are played with or without water, they have a few finger-holes, and there are even models which are both water-whistles and piggy-banks. Among the known places of production, we can name Torhout, Schellebelle, Leuven, Nimy and Sirault.

The *rommelpot** ('grumble-pot'), a friction drum, is connected to the liturgical calendar. It is usually an earthen pot closed by a stretched pig's bladder, in the middle of which is tied a small rod which one rubs with a damp hand or a dampened cloth. The oldest known representation is in a painting by Pieter Bruegel the Elder. There are many local Flemish names: *goebe*, *foekepot*, *prospot*. In Wallonia, it used to be found only around the village of Aubel.

The rituals of the carnival season have spawned a series of noise-makers like the 'Harlequin's bat', known in Wallonia as the *clatchârd*, and as *klepperlat* in the Flemish community. There are also various kinds of scrapers* which resemble stylised violins. In the centre of the structure is an opening containing moveable wooden or metal blades, which one scrapes with a toothed stick. Other bowed instruments are also used especially at carnival time, like the pseudo-basses. These are shaped like boards or broomsticks and

19. Pieter Bruegel the Elder (c. 1525-1569), *The fight between Carnival and Lent*, **1559.**
© Kunsthistorisches Museum Wien

This painting is the oldest Flemish representation of a *rommelpot* player. It may be supposed that the instrument was brought to the Low Countries by the Spanish occupiers.

20. Scraper-rattle, Brussels, 19th century
(inv. M2271)

Cut from beechwood and decorated in polychrome, this instrument was played with a toothed stick (absent on this photo) and was used by the *Cercle de Bultkarkas*, a group of punchinellos in Brussels.

are strung with a piece of rope and a pig's bladder for resonance. They were especially popular in the 17th and 18th centuries. Then there is the clog-fiddle, a crude imitation of a violin made from a clog. Last but not least, there are the many varieties of rattles, scrapers and castanets known in Wallonia as *brouya*, *clabot*, *crakète*, *maka*, *ragalète*, *rahia*, *tarata*, and in Flanders as *ratelaar*, *krekelaar*, *klepper* and *iktik*.

11. Ensembles and playing in ensembles

The iconography of the 15th and 16th centuries is full of scenes showing musicians playing together. However, the musical life of the times is not always accurately reflected. Many documents have only a symbolic significance, often taking a moral stance, or are simply a visual inventory of the instruments of the day.

Up until around the middle of the 16th century the visual arts concentrated mainly on courtly scenes. Wind and stringed instruments can be seen being played alongside one another in ensembles. Stringed instruments are not seen in scenes of tournaments or rowdy hunting parties. A little later we can see small groups playing at weddings and village fairs. Usually these were duos — transverse flute and drum, bagpipe accompanied by the hurdy-gurdy or the fiddle, sometimes a bass fiddle, a tambourine, or even a pseudo-bass would be added to these small ensembles. From the middle of the 16th century onwards we begin to see town musicians taking part in parades and

21. Ensemble from the surroundings of Brussels, c. 1900. Collection Gildenkamer van Midden-Brabant

The following instruments can be seen: violin, single action accordion (German model), triangle, cello and two tin whistles.

processions. Their ensembles were made up of wind instruments — trumpets, trombones, shawms, bombardes, cornetts and dulcians. Ensembles of these instruments are often mentioned in archive material and furthermore can be seen — for once as accurate representations — in the paintings of Antoon Sallaert (1590-1658), which show the Brussels *Ommegang* pageants, religious processions and shooting competitions.

From the end of the 18th century, and particularly from 1830 onwards, wind bands and brass bands began to appear in the majority of towns and villages. Then a variety of other instruments also began to make their entrance into the dance orchestras — the clarinet, the valve cornet and the lower brass instruments such as the baritone and the tuba. These groups were extraordinarily successful and as a result many village musicians received a musical training, some were even able to write down and to arrange their repertoire. From this moment on we can see a remarkable development in the written musical tradition. Numerous musical notebooks have been kept dating from the 19th century and from the first half of the 20th century which contain arrangements of dance tunes. In these arrangements, often made by village musicians, we can see almost all the different types of traditional ensemble groups. The well made orchestrations often contain one or more polyphonic themes or long passages. The part of each instrument is very clearly defined.

In the new folk bands the brass instruments only have a limited role, whereas the violin, clarinet, flute and accordion are very important. Many groups still use traditional instruments such as the plucked dulcimer, the bagpipe, the hurdy-gurdy and the fife.

12. Further matters...

A whole host of instruments and 'noise makers' fall outside our thematic classification. This is the case, for example, of the xylophone, also known as the *claquebois* ('strike wood') in French, or *strovedel* ('straw fiddle') in Flemish. This instrument, which has been played since the 17th century, is made of a number of wooden bars of graduated length placed on narrow straw supports. The xylophone used to be a real attraction in dance orchestras, as were the 'musical bottles', a dozen or so bottles filled with water, which could produce specific musical notes. These were suspended side by side from a string stretched between two uprights, and were played with two felt drumsticks. Instruments such as glass horns and trumpets* do not have a musical function; they were made by Walloon glass blowers. The manufacture of these purely aesthetic creations ceased after the First World War.

22. Three glass trumpets and one horn, Wallonia, end of the 19th and beginning of the 20th century (inv. 3543, HB141, HB140 & HB216)

The trumpet on the left is in green and zinc coloured glass, that in the middle in white glass, the trumpet on the right in blue glass and the horn in white glass. Most of these instruments were made in workshops of Lodelinsart and Chênée.

An instrument that used to be played solely in rural peasant communities is the cow horn, used mainly by cowherds for communicating. Bells can also be found in a whole variety of forms, many have been preserved that date from the Gallo-Roman period. Bells have always been attached to horse harnesses but they also had other uses. A good example of this is the *apertintaille*, a large belt hung with small bronze bells and worn by the famous *Gilles* of Binche and surrounding villages.

Finally, we should not forget the numerous bird call devices used for attracting and capturing birds, and also the huge variety of children's toys. Of these toys the fingerclappers were surely the most highly prized. They were made of two simple pieces of hard wood and were considered to be the castanets of the old Low Countries. They appeared in Belgium at the end of the 16th century, but they ceased to be played during the Second World War. Over the last few years they have begun to reappear and are remarkably popular.

EUROPEAN
FOLK INSTRUMENTS

A word of introduction

There are some 270 instruments on display in the section of popular European instruments, all of which were part of the musical life of the common people. In fact, this way of formulating such categories is somewhat artificial, as it is very difficult to draw a distinct line in music between Asia and Europe, or between the upper classes and the folk. Regions such as Anatolia or the Caucasus, which are generally included in Asia, are real unifying forces between the musical cultures of the East and the West; this is why they have a place here.

Moreover, there are several instruments amongst those exhibited here that were played across all the social classes. In fact the distinction between 'folk' and 'art' music was made only from the Romantic era onwards, and it would be wrong to believe that they are two completely distinct types of music. There are many cases in which we can see that the music of one social class has an influence on that of another. It would though be true to say that the folk often tend to keep instruments, or tend to enjoy types of music long after they have gone out of fashion in more elite circles. In other words, bagpipes, hurdy-gurdies, lutes and fiddles were once also heard in the houses of the aristocracy.

The cultural heritage of European folk instruments is remarkably varied. There are many regional differences in construction, repertoire, playing technique and distribution of the instruments.

13. Lutes and fiddles, or the journey from Asia to Europe

Europe is particularly rich in folk instruments, but — give honour where honour is due — much of this richness is owed to the East. Prior to the 8th century the greater part of Europe would probably only have known small flutes, horns, trumpets and plucked instruments without a neck, such as harps and lyres. Plucked stringed instruments on which the strings were held down and which had a neck extending from the sound box, i.e. the lute family in the largest sense, were first seen more than 4,000 years ago with the Semites in Syria. These instruments reached the Mediterranean basin even before our time. However, they only really became established in Europe by the 8th century, thanks to contact with the Byzantine and Moorish cultures.

The lute family is divided into two main groups: the short-necked lute and the long-necked lute. The short-necked lute, derived from the Arab *ud*, played an important part in popular music during the Middle Ages, particularly in Western Europe. By the Renaissance, however, it had become a symbol of the bourgeoisie. The Romanian and Moldavian *cobza* is the only short-necked lute to have maintained a place in popular European music. The family of long-necked lutes* is far more varied, even though it is largely restricted to the east and south of Europe. The long-necked lutes are often used to accompany a vocal part or another instrument.

23. *Tar*, **Nagorno-Karabakh, Caucasus, beginning of the 20th century** (inv. 97.023)

The bow also originated in Central Asia. It was introduced into Europe in the 11th century, also through Byzantium and Moorish Spain. The medieval fiddle survived mainly in the Balkans and the Greek islands*. Elsewhere, since the 16th century, it has largely been replaced by the violin, which is still one of the favourite instruments of the village musicians.

24. Kosta Vassilarakis, *lyra* **player, and Nikos Vlachos,** *laouto* **player, Othos, Island of Karpathos, Greece, 1998.** Photo Ritteke Demeulenaere

14. The plucked dulcimer: a domestic musical instrument

In certain regions, even well into the 20th century, the plucked dulcimer was practically the only folk instrument played by women and young girls. This is due to the fact that it is mainly associated with the family and the home. It has never been an instrument played by (semi)professional village musicians. The instrument has an elongated sound box, often in the shape of a log. In some cases this is fixed onto a second, larger box, which may be pear shaped, or similar to an elongated guitar. As is typical of a domestic instrument, the plucked dulcimer can be found in a whole range of shapes and sizes. There are examples of quite primitive instruments in which the body is roughly fashioned from a single block of wood, and equally there are examples of highly skilful works of real craftsmanship. Two series of strings are stretched the length of the body: one series of melody strings and one series of drones. The melody strings are tuned in unison and pass over a range of frets that are usually diatonic. The Hungarian *citera* often has a second range of frets, which complete the chromatic series. The plucked dulcimer is usually played on the knees or on a table. The strings are pressed against the frets with the aid of a stick or with the fingers of the left hand, and are plucked with a plectrum or the fingers of the right hand. The building and the playing techniques vary according to local traditions.

The plucked dulcimer probably comes from Scandinavia. The oldest known representation can be seen on a fresco dating from around 1560 in the church

25. Ragna Brenno Frydenberg, *langeleik* player, Valdres, Norway.
Norsk Folkemuseum, Oslo

26. Zither, Tyrol, Austria, before 1880 (inv. M527)

of Rynkeby on the Danish island of Fyn. An instrument was even found in Norway inscribed with the date 1524. The instrument was popular throughout Central and Western Europe, particularly in Germanic countries and their neighbours, but not in the British Isles. The oldest Dutch example dates from 1608.

The plucked dulcimer is still very popular in the Vosges (*épinette des Vosges*), in Norway (*langeleik**) and in Hungary (*citera*). Scandinavian and German emigrants took their instruments with them to the Appalachians (USA) where it became known as the *dulcimer*. In the German speaking part of the Alps the zither* evolved during the 19th century from an archaic drone instrument into a sophisticated instrument capable of a whole range of melodic and harmonic possibilities. The melodic strings are tuned at different pitches and are shortened only by the fingers. The frets are totally chromatic and there are often more than forty accompanying strings.

15. Different types of stringed instruments

Here we have another illustration of the remarkable diversity of stringed instruments, be they plucked, struck or bowed, in European folk music. In the Baltic countries and in Russia the psalteries, with plucked strings, still play a major part in traditional music. In Finland in the 19th century, the *kantele* even rose to the status of a national symbol. The Russian psaltery, the *gusli*, is distinguished from its Baltic cousin mainly by the symmetrical layout of the strings. The *crwth* is a type of Welsh lyre. When the bow was introduced into Europe, it was also used on lyres of this type.

In most of Europe the violin replaced the older bowed instruments, but in Scandinavia two bowed instruments resisted the change. The Norwegian *hardingfele** has four or five sympathetic strings. The *nyckelharpa* of Sweden is a fiddle with a system of keys similar to that of the hurdy-gurdy.

The hurdy-gurdy* and the dulcimer probably both came from the East during the 12th century, the hurdy-gurdy through Moorish Spain, and the dulcimer

27. *Hardingfele*, **Norway, repaired and embellished by J.C.L. Ruwold in 1812** (inv. M1329)

in the luggage of Flemish Crusaders. Interestingly, it is only in Europe that the hurdy-gurdy is still known, and this has been the case over many centuries. It was once widespread, apart from in the Balkans, and is still very popular in Central France.

Unlike the psaltery, on which the strings are plucked, the strings on the dulcimer are struck by small hammers. This instrument became popular throughout a large part of Europe. Nowadays it survives mainly in England and in Central and Eastern Europe.

The *gardon*, which is often in the shape of the cello, is only played in the Hungarian Székely community, in North-East Romania, where it is used to accompany the fiddle. This instrument is of note because the strings are alternately plucked then hit by a stick.

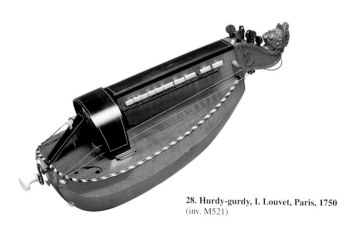

28. Hurdy-gurdy, I. Louvet, Paris, 1750 (inv. M521)

16. Horns and trumpets: instruments for calling and for magic

Blowing into an animal horn* or into a shell belongs to the very earliest of human musical experiences. The horns and the trumpets (there is no clear unanimity in the definition of these terms), are also often made from a slender trunk. This is cut in half along its length and the two halves are hollowed out before being reunited under strips of bark or other binding. From the Bronze Age onwards metal was also used to make horns and trumpets. The bronze *lurs* found in the peat bogs of the Baltic are amongst the oldest European instruments to have survived. The example on display is a copy.

Horns and trumpets were used above all as calling instruments. They were a major means of communication by shepherds, particularly in mountainous regions. The spectacular Swiss *alphorn* is the most well-known example, but it is by no means the only one. Horns and trumpets had a similar function in the Carpathian mountains — the Romanian *trîmbita* and *bucium* are good examples.

Horns and trumpets were obvious signalling instruments in the army. The Roman legions marched into battle to the sound of *lituus*, *buccina*, *cornu* and *tuba*. Their raucous, strident sounds were intended both to galvanise the soldiers into action and to scare off the enemy. In addition they were supposed to chase away evil spirits. Blowing into horns or trumpets was also a way of breathing new life into Nature. The *midwinterhoorn**, which can

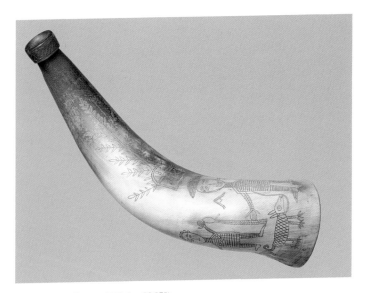

29. Cow horn, France, 1854 (inv. 90.070)

30. *Midwinterhoorn* **player, Twente, Overijssel, The Netherlands, c. 1950.**
Collection E.A. Meyling

still be heard at Advent in Twente in the Netherlands, undoubtedly has a similar magical origin.

On the whole horns do not have finger holes, the sounds produced are therefore only harmonics.

17. The friction drum: a calendar instrument

In Europe there is no instrument as closely linked with the popular calendar as the friction drum. European friction drums consist of a container sealed by a membrane. In the middle of the membrane there is a stick, for example a piece of reed, or a strand of horsehair, which is rubbed with the hands.

The friction drum is first seen in 15th century Spanish sources. It is also equally well known in various forms in many parts of Black Africa. It is quite possible that the instrument came to the Iberian peninsula after exploratory voyages to the West coast of Africa, or with the black slaves who were deported in the 15th century.

The friction drum can be seen principally in three specific areas:
- The Iberian peninsula and neighbouring Occitania;
- The Low Countries, North-West Germany and Jutland;
- The Ukraine, Moldavia, Romania, Hungary, Eastern Serbia, Slovenia, Carinthia, the Czech Republic and Slovakia.

It is played mainly by people collecting money from house to house in the period between Christmas and Twelfth Night, and also for Shrove Tuesday.

31. *Fanfrnoch*, Klenèi, Bohemia, Czechoslovakia, **1988** (inv. HB231)

32. *Rommelpot* players, Liempde, North Brabant, the Netherlands, c. **1930-1940.** MIM, Brussels; photo D.J. van der Ven

In the east and the south of Europe the instrument can sometimes be heard in peasant dance orchestras. In Hungary *citera* ensembles are often accompanied by a friction drum.

18. The rim-blown flute: a pastoral instrument

In every era, in every place, shepherds and goatherds have always been important keepers of the musical tradition of their community. The reason is all too obvious: there is no other occupation that entails such a degree of solitude. There is an additional advantage to making music: it keeps the animals calm and prevents them from straying from the shepherd; it is also said to improve milk production. Herdsmen have a great preference for wind instruments: horns, flutes and reed instruments, such as the bagpipe were the preferred instrument. Usually they make the instruments themselves from animal or vegetable materials that they have to hand.

The rim-blown flute is quite typical of the pastoral tradition. It is a long cylindrical tube, open at both ends. The upper rim is bevelled. The player holds the flute at a slight angle and blows against the rim. It takes considerable practice to master the technique. Some rim-blown flutes, such as the Romanian *tilinca*, do not have any holes. Harmonics can be produced by varying breath pressure, and by opening or closing the distal end with the forefinger.

However, six or seven holed flutes, with or without a thumb hole, are more widespread. A pair of *kaval*, tuned in unison, (*tšift kavali*), is typically found in Macedonia and is kept together in a case or a sheath.

33. Kostadin Petrov Kunev, *kaval* **player, Babuk, Dobrudzha, Bulgaria, 1965.**
Photo Vergilii Atanassov

Rim-blown flutes can be found only in Southeastern Europe, from continental Greece to the Ukrainian Carpathians. Flutes which are from 60 to 80cm long are almost always called kaval* (*kafal, kaváli*), a name taken from the Turks, as is the instrument itself. The short flutes, however, have their own names according to their origins: *šupelka* (Macedonia), *floyéra* (Greece), *fluier* (Romania), *floyar** (Ukrainian Carpathians), etc.

34. From left to right: Mykhaylo (*floyar*) and Yuryi Tafyichuk (*tsimbaly*), Verkhnyi Iaseniv, Carpathian Mountains, Ukraine, 1992. Photo Hubert Boone

19. The panpipes: a mythical instrument

An ancient Greek myth tells how Pan, the God of forests and fields, went in pursuit of the naiad Syrinx, with whom he had fallen in love. Just as they were to meet on the banks of the Ladon, she was turned into a clump of reeds by Gaia, and as the wind blew, so was heard a sound like the melancholy lament of a flute. It was thus that a new musical instrument was born, an instrument that Pan would henceforth play in memory of his beloved Syrinx. Panpipes are amongst the earliest types of European flutes. They can be seen on some Hallstatt bronze urns from North-East Italy, which date from the 6th century B.C. The instrument spread throughout most of Europe, especially as a herdman's instrument. It should be noted that the panpipes disappeared from its original country, and that it is no longer found even in the Balkans. European panpipes can be divided into two categories: the first type, as in the

35. *Trstenke*, **Franc Laporšek, Haloze, Slovenia, c. 1990** (inv. 96.001)

36. The *I Bej firlinfeu* ensemble, Erba, Lombardy, Italy, c. 1995. Collection I Bej

Greek myth, consists of a row of straight pipes of different lengths, open at the top end and closed at the bottom. These pipes are held together in the form of a raft. Examples of this type are the Slovenian *trstenke** and the Romanian *nai*, which are both true musical instruments. In Lombardy *firlinfeu* orchestras* were begun during the 19th century for panpipes of different sizes, on the model of brass bands and wind bands. The second type of panpipe is smaller, made of a piece of hard wood with different sized holes. This type is seen particularly in the Iberian peninsula and in the French Pyrenees. It was used by goatherds and by travellers such as knife-grinders and peddlers, who played it to announce their arrival.

20. Terracotta whistles: from toy to musical instrument

From the Gallo-Roman period onwards, terracotta whistles have always been highly prized as toys by children all over Europe. They can be found in all manner of shapes and sizes, but are mainly in the form of a bird. This might be due to their original function in spring rituals.

These whistles are blown through a head with a mouth, as on a recorder. It is only possible to produce indeterminate notes, and not real tunes, even if there are finger-holes. Some whistles have to be partially filled with water and the sound then produced is a warbling noise similar to that of the nightingale. Some of them can also be used as a money box.

Towards 1865, Giuseppe Donati, of Budrio, near Bologna, took it into his head to turn these terracotta whistles into a proper musical instrument, thus inventing the ocarina*. 'Ocarina' means 'little goose' and refers to the shape of the instrument which resembles a stylised bird shape.

37. Terracotta whistles of different shapes and sizes: bird, France, 19th century; jug, Italy; peacock, Russia, 1990; horse, Slovenia, 1983; bird, Romania, 1990; ox's head, the Netherlands, before 1900; ocarina, Vienna, before 1893
(inv. HB167, HB032, 90.095, HB134, HB218, M2000 & M1007)

Ocarinas are usually made of clay, sometimes plastic or metal. The smallest model, which is also the most common, has ten holes, one for each finger. The pitch varies according to the total surface area of the open holes. Given that the resonator is egg-shaped and closed, it is not possible to overblow.

Ocarina playing is essentially an individual pastime, although they are occasionally heard in small dance or variety orchestras. At the height of their popularity, real ocarina bands were formed with instruments of all sizes, from bass to sopranino. Nowadays the ocarina is rarely more than a toy.

21. Different types of flutes

The most widely disseminated type of flute in Europe is the category of the duct flute, where the air is led through a narrow duct in the head of the tube, to the instrument's lip at the base of a mouth — thus relieving the player from the responsibility for directing the air flow.

The date of the first appearance of this type of flute in Europe is still the subject of a certain polemic: does it date from ancient prehistorical times, or was it introduced in the early Middle Ages? In Central and Northern Europe, the earliest extant duct flutes that can be confidently dated are from the 9th or 10th centuries.

Since duct flutes are easier to play than other flutes, they have long been popular as amateur's instruments. They appear in many different forms. They can have any number of holes up to ten — one for each finger — or no holes at all. They have been made from all kinds of material: tree-bark, bone, metal, even plastic, and, of course, wood. Since the 19th century, keys have sometimes been added. They can have either a conical or cylindrical bore, and can be as long as two meters, like the Slovakian *fujara**.

The double flute, like many other flutes, was a favourite of herdsmen

38. Karol Kočik (1964-), *fujara* player, Zvolen, Podpol'anie, Slovakia, 1986. Photo Tibor Szabó

39. *Dvojnice*, **Croatia, before 1879**
(inv. M191)

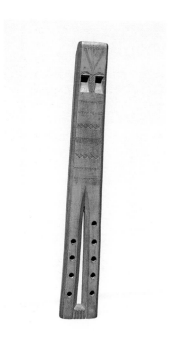

from the Balkans to the Carpathian mountains. In Macedonia, Bulgaria, Romania and Slovakia, it combines a melodic flute with a drone flute*. In the Balkans, both flutes have holes, which allows for two-voiced polyphonic music. In the Ukraine, we find both types of double flute.

The transverse flute came to the West by way of Byzantium in the 10th century notably as a herdsmen's instrument. In the mid-15th century, the flute and the drum became the favourite instruments of troops of mercenary soldiers in the Alpine regions. Subsequently, this type of music became very popular for parades and other open-air festivities in a large part of Western Europe.

22. The tabor pipe: a festive open-air instrument

In parts of Southwestern Europe, the drum and the tabor pipe are still popular instruments for outdoor festivities. Usually played with the left hand, this flute has two holes for fingers and another for the thumb, usually placed in the lower third of the tube. In spite of its simplicity, it has a wide range of musical possibilities. Because of its narrow cylindrical bore and the low position of the holes, it is possible to produce a harmonic series by overblowing, giving a complete diatonic scale with a range of up to an octave and a fifth.

Normally the player accompanies himself on a rhythmic instrument. In some parts of the Pyrenees like the Béarn and the province of Huesca we find a box zither*. It consists of an elongated resonator over which drone strings in any number from four up to ten are stretched. They are struck with a small stick. Elsewhere we find the flute accompanied by drums whose size varies from region to region. The tallest are to be found in Provence, where they are about 70cm in height and where they are called *tambourin*. The *galoubet* and *tambourin* are sometimes accompanied by a pair of *timbalons*; these are small kettledrums.

40. Player of the pipe and *tambourin du Béarn*, **Casteljaloux, Lot-et-Garonne, France, c. 1900. Post card.** From the collection of Hubert Boone

41. Tabor pipe, Delft, Holland, about 1375-1450 (inv. 95.036)

The combination of pipe and tabor is for the first time in history both visually represented and described in Spanish mid-13th century sources. In the Basque country and in Provence, the *txistu* and the *galoubet* respectively, have become national instruments. There is a flourishing tradition in some parts of Portugal, Western Spain and on the island of Ibiza. The Spanish colonisers of Latin America took the pipe and tabor with them. In England, the pipe and tabor are still used for the traditional morris dances.

The Catalan *flabiol* is a special case. It is a short flute with usually three holes on the front, but there are not one, but two holes underneath, one of which is stopped with the little finger. It is used in the *cobla* bands.

23. The oboe: a festive open-air instrument

The strident sound of the double reed makes of the oboe a perfect outdoors instrument. The most archaic type of oboe is the horn made of tree bark, which throughout Europe has the same appearance. This instrument produces only indeterminate sounds. Of oriental origin, the first European appearance of the oboe as a true melodic instrument was sometime in the 13th century. In Western Europe, it became one of the favourite instruments for all kinds of open-air festivities, especially in the cities. It was only in the 17th century that its sound became refined enough to use in indoor chamber music. In

42. *Piffero*, **Abruzzi region, Italy, before 1877** (inv. M181)

Northwestern Europe, the 'refined' oboe is now replaced for outdoor use by the wind bands that were current from the end of the 18th century. But the old outdoor oboes continued to be used in traditional music, especially in Southern Europe.

The oboe is rarely played alone, but often in a duo, either with a bagpipe (in Brittany and in Italy*) or with a drum (in Spain, the French Pyrenees, or in Languedoc). In Catalonia, we find the *tiple* and the *tenora* in the large *cobla* bands.

In Balkan traditional music, the oboe, called *zurna*, *zurla* or *zournás*, plays an important role. It is always accompanied by the large two-faced drum called

43. Left to right: Arsen Smabatian (*dhol***), Vladimir Smabatian (***parkapzuk***), Levon Hayrapetian (***duduk***), Armavir, Armenia, 1996.** Photo Hubert Boone

the *tapan* or *daoúli*. There is often also a second oboe, either playing a drone or occasional phrases with the soloist. The players, usually gypsies, use the technique of circular breathing to obtain a continuous sound. This technique consists of inhaling through the nose while maintaining the outward air flow with the mouth cavity.

The *zurna* is also common in Turkey and the Caucasus, where we also find another peculiar kind of oboe. This instrument is called *mey*, *duduk**, *balaman* or *balaban* and is closely related to the *monaulos* of ancient Greece. The peculiarity of this instrument is its enormous double reed and its cylindrical bore. Its sound is remarkably soft, reminding us of the clarinet, and it is thus an ideal indoor instrument.

24. Different types of drums and tambours

There are four principal types of European drum, categorized by their different forms: cylindrical, goblet-shaped, bowl-shaped, or built on a frame. The most common type is cylindrical, as in the side drum, the snare drum or the bass drum. Goblet-shaped drums are usually made in pottery. These and the bowl-shaped kettledrums are mainly used in the Caucasus, in Turkey and in the Balkan regions. But frame drums are found throughout Europe, and are possibly of prehistorical origin. They are usually round and are often fitted with jingles or small bells. The tambourine* is the most common example.

44. Tambourine, Florence, Italy, before 1900 (inv. M1951)

25. Clarinets

The air in a clarinet is set in vibration by a single reed. There are folk clarinets throughout Europe, but their role is generally much more modest than that of the oboe. In its simplest form, it is nothing more than the stem of a reed or an oat stalk into one end of which is cut a vibrating reed and in which holes are burnt. More often, the single reed is made separate and can therefore be replaced.

The ancient Greek *aulos* is nothing more than this type of instrument, with two reed pipes at a slight angle. The Sardinian *launeddas** is a direct descendant of the aulos, made of three reed pipes, two melodic and one drone. *Launeddas* players use the technique of continuous breathing

Hornpipes go back to pre-medieval times. They are named after their bell, which is made of an animal horn, or has a similar shape. Hornpipes often have two joined parallel melodic pipes. Examples are the Russian *zhaleyka* and the Basque *alboka*, the last surviving type of hornpipe in Western Europe. Most folk clarinets are made from natural materials that the maker can easily find in his environment. Sometimes the reeds are covered by wind cap. In the case of hornpipes this is often made from a piece of animal horn.

The early bagpipe is clearly derived from similar antique clarinets. Some double clarinets, like the Croatian *diple*, are blown either directly by the player's breath or through a bag.

45. Luigi Lai, player of the *launeddas*, San Vito, Sardinia, 1998. Photo Dirk Veulemans

46. *Tárogató*, V.J. Schunda, Budapest, **before 1922** (inv. M3267)

The *tárogató** is a singular type of clarinet; it is made with the conical bore typical of the oboe, but it is played with a single reed. It was developed in the Budapest workshop of V. József Schunda in 1894-1896, and became immediately very popular both in Hungary and in certain nearby regions.

26. The bagpipe: from the shepherds' pasture to the salon

It is believed that the bagpipe was already known in ancient Greece and Rome. Perhaps the Emperor Nero himself is the first historically recognised bagpiper. But, surprisingly enough, we possess no iconographic evidence of this instrument before the 13th century.

Until the turn of the 20th century, bagpipes were in use in practically all of Europe. Like the flute, it was herdsmen who had a particular penchant for the instrument. In other parts of society, it evoked the most diverse reactions: it was both detested as a devilish instrument, and found worthy to entertain the aristocracy.

In its simplest form the bagpipe consists of a blowpipe, a bag and a chanter with a single or double reed. The bag can be made of an animal's bladder, as in the Chuvash *shapar* or the Cheremiss *shuvyr*, but is usually in leather. In Central and Southeastern Europe a whole sheep- or goatskin is often used. The pipes are attached at the holes once occupied by the neck and the legs of the animal*. Elsewhere the bags are simply sewn leather.

There are two main types of melodic pipes or chanters: the conical oboe-type bore, found in the British Isles and from Germany to Spain, and elsewhere, the cylindrical clarinet-type bore. But there are always exceptions: the Italian *zampogna* has conical clarinets, and the *musette de cour* and the Northumberland small-pipes are cylindrical oboes. In some regions bagpipes

47. *Duda* **player, Buják, Nógrád, Hungary, c. 1930.**
Budapest Ethnographic Museum

48. Andonis Zografidis, *tsambouna* **player, Olympos, Karpathos Island, Greece, 1998.** MIM, Brussels. Photo Wim Bosmans

The musician is playing an instrument that he himself made and that is now on display in the MIM (inv. 98.015).

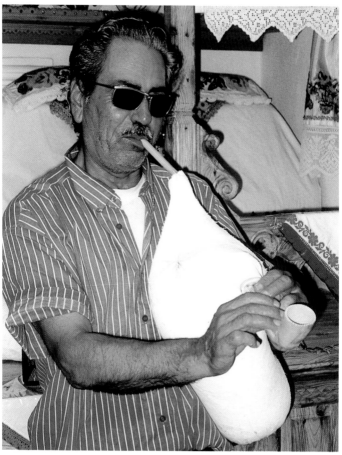

49. Jeanty Benquet, *boha* **player, Bazas, Gironde, France, 1937.** English Folk Dance and Song Society, London

50. Uilleann pipes player, Ireland, c. 1900. National Library of Ireland, Lawrence Collection, Dublin

have a double chanter: Central and Southern Italy, the Croatian and Bosnian sea-coast, the Greek islands, the republics of the Volga and Northeastern Anatolia,.

Most instruments have one to three drones, usually clarinets with a cylindrical bore. In Hungary, Slovakia and the surrounding areas, bagpipes have a second *kontra*-pipe next to the main melodic chanter. This pipe is pierced with a single finger-hole; when stopped, it lowers the pitch by a fourth. These jumps have mainly a rhythmic function. Strikingly, the same bagpipes are found in the *Landes* in Gascony*, nearly 1,500 kilometers from Hungary.

In many countries bagpipes have remained unchanged since the Middle Ages. With the advent of the baroque style in Western Europe, however, some professional makers began looking for technical improvements that would render the instrument apt to the performance of the new style, and would thus appeal to the upper classes. Around 1600, the idea of furnishing the bagpipe with bellows came to the fore in France, and it was also adopted in the British Isles and in Central Europe. In the 17th century, the French *musette de cour* was given keys, thus chromatic semitones were possible; also a system of little drawers allowed the pitch of the drones to be changed so that the instrument could be played in different keys. On the Irish uilleann pipes*, the player can activate keys placed on the chord pipes — known as regulators — with his wrist, making this instrument the only bagpipe that can play chords.

27. Idiophones

This class of instruments are those which are played by striking, shaking, scraping, rubbing, pounding, or simply knocking them against each other. Any hard object is a potential idiophone, such as two kitchen spoons, which can be played with remarkable rhythmic virtuosity. Castanets* belong to this family, and are found especially on the Iberian peninsula; they are also to be played in France and Italy. Pairs of fingerclappers, known as *cliquettes*, made of either wood or bone, are used mainly in Western Europe. In Catholic communities, clappers and rattles replace bells during Holy Week. Bells are used for many kinds of general communications, quite apart from church use. We still find herds of sheep, goats or cattle carrying bells in mountain pastures.

51. *Castañolas*, Ibiza, Spain, before 1900
(inv. M1935)

Small globular bells are frequently used for rhythmic purposes. They are often part of traditional carnival costumes and they are also worn for ritual dances such as the English morris dances. They are attached to the *lozhki*, a typically Russian instrument used by the cavalry in music inspired by the Janissaries.

28. The Jew's harp: a pastime instrument

This universally known instrument is played to pass the time. In Sicily and in Austria, it was used to serenade young ladies. In Europe, there are pictures and mentions of the Jew's harp already in the 14th century, and in some archaeological digs examples are found that are probably older. Originally made by the village blacksmith, from the 16th century the instrument was produced in large numbers for export, especially in Upper Austria, where the village of Molln is well known among connoisseurs.

52. Jew's harps, England, before 1900
(inv. M2549/8 & inv. M1944)

29. The accordion: a newcomer

At the end of the 18th century, musicians and physicists were fascinated by Far Eastern mouth-organs, like the Chinese *cheng* or the Japanese *sho*. From these curiosities a whole new family of free reed instruments was created in the first decades of the 19th century. The free reed consists of a metal tongue in a frame which allows it to vibrate when blown. The air source can be from a human mouth (the harmonica), or a bellows (the accordion or the harmonium).

In 1829, the accordion was patented by a Viennese builder named Zyril Demian: it was the first accordion that had both melodic keys and keys that played chords. Between 1830 and 1860, Paris was the centre of accordion making. Instruments in this period were made by hand from sophisticated materials. They were thus exclusively for the wealthy classes.

53. Accordion, Paris, c. 1850-1860 (inv. HB215)

At the end of the 19th century, especially in Italy and in Germany, mass-production was undertaken. The resulting drop in price as well as the possibility to play melodies, harmonies, bass lines and rhythm on an instrument requiring virtually no tuning or maintenance contributed to the instrument's popularity, and it came to be used by the folk musicians throughout Europe, except in the Ottoman Empire.

Unlike the accordion, the English concertina has no keys which play chords. The double action English concertina, which has a typical hexagonal case, was patented by the Englishman Charles Wheatstone in 1844. Ten years earlier, the German builder Carl Friedrich Uhlig had already conceived a single action *Konzertina* with a square shape. In 1846, Heinrich Band modified this instrument and produced the *bandoneon*. This instrument became the backbone of Argentinian tango orchestras and later developed into single rank variants.

54. Concertina, Lachenal, London, c. 1900 (inv. 4205)

INSTRUMENTS
FROM OUTSIDE EUROPE

30. African harps and lyres

Harps and lyres, known from the beginning of history, are still to be found virtually unchanged in some parts of Africa. Arched harps similar to those seen in representations from the Egyptian Ancient Empire and the Middle Empire, are still in use by the Zande people in Northern Congo. The Ethiopian *krar** is a survivor of the ancient Greek lyre and the *beganna*, from Ethiopia, is built like the Greek *kithara*.

Arched harps of the Zande people, the *kundi**, are prized for their beautiful exterior finishing. They are used to accompany the poetry sung by professional musicians. Through the years, the string material has evolved from liana to palm-tree fibers to gut to nylon. Today, nylon is preferred for its stability. The instrument usually has five strings. It is hung high in the hut, where over time it becomes covered with a patina of soot.

The *kora**, a harp lute or harp with a bridge, can be found in Senegal, Gambia, Guinea, Mali and Burkina Faso. A *kora* usually has twenty-one leather strings. It is the favourite instrument for accompanying the *griots*. These are bards who are either in the service of a high-placed person or who move from clan to clan offering their services. The griots adapt their praises according to their employer. Their ancient poetry consists of the oral history

55. *Krar* **(lyre), Ethiopia** (inv. M390)

56. *Kundi* **(arched harp), Zande, Congo** (inv. 73.009)

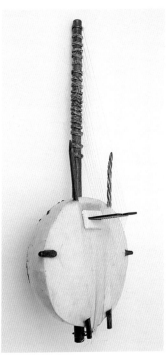

57. *Kora* (harp lute), Senegal-Gambia
(inv. 3421)

of the tribe or people. They also participate actively in the solemn rituals. Some griots have developed a highly virtuoso style and are unashamed about showing it off.

The *pluriarc* is basically a multiple musical bow on a single body. It is not a member of the harp family, but is classified as a type of lute. It is used very differently according to the region. In the coastal and equatorial regions of Congo, it is used to accompany singing. In other regions, it is used in hunting rituals, or for accompanying dancing, stimulating warriors or praising the tribal chieftain.

31. Talking drums

From the point of view of Western culture, music does not have a semantic content: no precise information is communicated; music elicits rather vague feelings. But in Asian, South American and African cultures, music is often used to communicate a precise message.

The *talking drum* can either be a skin drum, a wooden drum or a slit drum*. The essential quality of this instrument is that it be capable of producing two distinct pitches. In the case of skin drums, one uses either a pair of drums, or a double-faced drum, often in the shape of an hour-glass.

In Africa, information is coded in a rhythmical succession of high sounds (-) and low sounds (_). For instance the word for moon, *songe* in the language of the Kele people of the Congo is represented by two high sounds (--). In the language of the drums, 'songe li tange la manga' becomes '- - _ - _ _ _ _', meaning 'the moon looks down upon the earth'. In Oceania, the binary system uses long and short signals. The *teponatzle*, a meter-long slit drum, is one of the most important instruments of the Aztecs. It has survived from ancient times and is still in use in Mexico.

58. Slit drum in the shape of a seal,
Oceania (inv. IDK029)

32. African orchestras of wind instruments

In Africa, both trumpets and flutes are used as signalling devices and as means of communication as well as for making music. For music making, one finds instruments of different sizes in a group, each instrument producing a single note. Melodies are produced by group synchronisation, often using very complex rhythms.

Flute ensembles of this type are to be found especially in Eastern and Southern Africa. Ensembles of horns are used in the Ivory Coast, in Central Africa and around the Great Lakes. *Gbofi* is the name used by the Senufo of the Ivory Coast for their official orchestra of horns*. It consists of seven horns and two drums and is used mostly for representations. All these horns have lateral mouthpieces.

Senufo cosmology with musical instruments

'Once upon a time, the frogs played our *gbofi* horns, and it was the mice who played the xylophones called *dyegbahariga*. One day, the kite was after the frogs and the mice; he was lying beneath a tree pretending to be dead. In order to attract the flies he rubbed himself with the powder of the bark of a *néré* tree. The hare, who had taught him the trick, ran to tell the mice and the frogs, 'All come this way, the kite is dead!' The animals began to prepare for the funeral. The frogs went to get their *gbofi* horns and marched, playing:
Today we dance the dance of youth!
Then it was the turn of the mice, who proceeded in with their *dyegbahariga* xylophones, playing:
He who slaughtered us one by one
Now he lies dead beneath the tree!
The frogs and the mice came together and followed the funeral dance around the pretender:
Today we dance the dance of youth!
He who slaughtered us one by one
Now he lies dead beneath the tree!

59. Senufo metal and wood horns, Ivory Coast
(inv. 75.044/1, 75.044/2, 82.014 & 75.005/2)

The hare sprang into the dancing circle, lifted the kite's wing, and said 'Did I not tell you that he is indeed dead?' Still dancing, the frogs and the mice came close to the hawk who suddenly leapt up and grabbed them. The frogs who escaped into a nearby pool, and the mice who could dash into their holes had to abandon their instruments. The hare went to call men who came and took the instruments.

It was thus that humans were introduced to horns and xylophones' (noted down by Hugo Zemp in the 1960s).

33. Stringed instruments in the Indian sub-continent

The rich history of this ancient part of the world can be seen reflected in the incredible variety of stringed instruments still in use there, both in the music of the people and in the highly sophisticated music of the upper classes. For a Westerner, the most striking phenomenon is that many instruments have sympathetic strings. These vibrate freely, in resonance with the strings which are plucked or bowed by the player.

In India, there is a clear distinction between Hindustani music in the north and Carnatic music in the south. The Hindustani tradition comes principally from the muslim culture, brought by successive invaders from the West. The sitar* and the tabla* are the principal instruments of the north. The sitar is probably the invention of the 17th century Amir Khusrau of Delhi, but confusion with the name of a famous poet led players to claim that the instrument had its origins in the 12th century. The sitar is usually played together with the tabla and a drone instrument, the *tambūrā**; they are also used to accompany dances. The *sūrbahār* is a larger sitar, sounding at a lower pitch.

In north India, instruments had an important part to play in the classical vocal tradition. The *khyal* is one of the vocal styles, performed in princely courts

60. *Tambūrā* **and sitar (long-necked lutes), and tabla (pair of small drums), North India** (inv. 3919, 74.021/14 & 3926/27)

61. Shri Kumar Khan playing the *sindhī sārangī,* **Jodhpur, c. 1960.** MIM, Brussels; photo Ferdinand-Joseph De Hen

since the 19th century. The singer is accompanied by one or two *sārangī**, a tabla, and one or two *tambūrā*. The traditional patrons, who supported whole dynasties of musicians, have largely disappeared, and consequently the *sārangī* is being played less and less in modern India.

The stick zither, called *ekatantri vīnā*, a plucked instrument used since the 9th century, has a gourd for resonance. This ancient instrument is found in both the north and in the south of the sub-continent. The *rudra vīnā*, used in the north, has seven metal plucked strings and eighteen frets. Like the sitar, it rests on the player's shoulder. Since the 19th century, the vīnā has been largely supplanted by the sitar, basically a long-necked lute with a gourd body, especially for virtuoso solo music.

In the south the instrument is called the *saraswati vīnā*. Its music has not come under Muslim influence, and maintains a direct connection with a very ancient tradition. The curved harps are the oldest stringed instrument of India. They have completely disappeared from use, but we find a derivative instrument in Burma, the *saùng-gauk*.

The most widespread instrument on the sub-continent is the *ektārā*. It is a single-stringed spike lute with a gourd resonator, and is used above all by wandering mendicant monks.

34. Chinese opera

In Chinese opera, the actor himself is the creator. He must be a master of music, of drama, of song, of mime and of acrobatics. The principal subject of Chinese opera is the strife between good and evil, and it always ends with the most elevated sentiment vanquishing evil. Its popularity to this day has not waned, in spite of the Cultural Revolution, during which only eight operas were tolerated.

The music varies from place to place in its tonal systems, its temperament, its structure and its character. However, across these regional differences, we often find the same instruments. Fingerclappers and rattles emphasize the different psychological nuances of the characters. A gong is used for dramatic effect in scenes of combat. Small drums and tambourines underly and punctuate the singing. The flutist often evokes natural scenes. He leads the musicians, seconded by the oboe player. The great ballads and the skilful singing of the principal actors are accompanied by long-necked fiddles and a tambourine. The *pipa*, a plucked short-necked lute, accompanies only specific songs.

'What do we hear, shrieking from radios playing full blast in any self-respecting shop which can afford one in Peking, Mukden, Shanghai or Canton? Opera arias. Taxi drivers waiting for fares, what are they humming when one strolls by? Opera arias. When company commanders or officials of

62. *Bo* (cymbals), *suona* (oboe), two *di* (transverse flutes), China
(inv. M646, M698, M725, M730 & M291)

63. *Yueqin* (pointed lute), *tiqin* and *jinghu* (short-necked fiddles), China
(inv. M1923, M146 & M145)

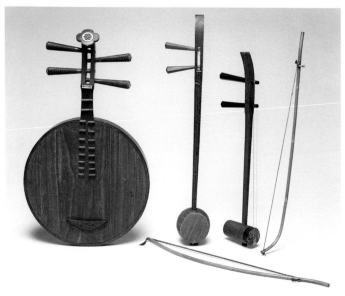

remote villages need to explain a strategic principle, or to clarify the purpose of a manoeuvre, to what do they quite naturally refer? To the great novels, both classical and popular, of China. Perhaps everyone has not read them, but they all know the heroes, the intrigues, the details of the plots, because they have all seen them in the theatre' (Claude Roy).

64. Chinese musicians at the International Health Exhibition, London, 1884.
MIM, Brussels

35. A Mexican orchestra

Well before the Spanish conquest of Mexico, music was a major feature in native societies. Popular orchestras are still numerous throughout the country, and instrument-making is strikingly diverse.

Music is mainly made in groups, with singers and dancers. Formations are chosen for specific repertoires, but in all bands the instruments are divided according to three functions. The melody is played by a fiddle, flute or trumpet, guitars provide rhythmic and harmonic support, and the rhythm is reinforced by struck, shaken or scraped idiophones.

All the stringed instruments are Iberian in origin. The guitar family is highly varied in size, form, construction material, string disposition, etc. The *jarana** is a small five-stringed guitar. The *charango* is characterised by the convex form of its body (often made from an armadillo carapace) and by its five doubled strings. Now rare in Mexico, this instrument is still popular in South America. The *armadillo** owes its name to the animal whose carapace is used as a sound-box. It is distinguished from the *charango* by the length of its neck and its four paired strings. The *guitarrón** is an enormous six-stringed bass guitar, typical in *mariachi* bands. Its player stands holding the instrument against his belly.

Some chordophones, such as the tympanon and the harp*, on the other hand, have become rarer. The harp, which used to provide harmonic accompaniment to church choirs, was gradually replaced in the 18th century by the organ. In the 19th and 20th centuries its usage has become limited to rural folk bands.

The *marimba*, a xylophone probably introduced by African slaves, gives a unique colour to Southern Mexican orchestras.

65. *Guitarrón* (**bass guitar**), *armadillo* (**guitar with four courses**), **and** *jarana* (**five-stringed guitar**), **Mexico** (inv. 83.005, LS51 & 72.045)

Mariachi groups

The ensemble most commonly found in Mexican cities is the *mariachi* (probably from *Maria* and the diminutive *chi* in the Náhuatl language). Originally this formation included two violins, a *vihuela* (a small five-stringed guitar), a *jarana* and a harp. During the 20th century the harp was replaced by the *guitarrón*, more easily transported. Two trumpets were added in the 1930s, and it is in this form that *mariachi* bands are now popular in Mexico and throughout the world, thanks to the international media.

Half-breed and native traditions

Musically, the half-breed and native popular traditions co-existing in Mexico are not very different. What separates them in reality is economics; the Indians' resources are limited both by their geographic isolation and their barter economy. Their acquisition of instruments is made rarely by purchase, and more often by inheritance, trade or local making. The *jarana* illustrated is probably a locally-made copy of the half-breed instrument. The figure-of-eight shape of the calabash that forms its sound box recalls that of the *jarana*.

66. Players of harp and twelve-string guitar, Mexico, c. 1960.
MIM, Brussels; photo Johan Van Dijck

36. The gamelan or Indonesian gong ensemble

Gong ensembles are typical of South-East Asia but are also found in regions further away. They date from before the Christian era. According to some experts, gongs have always been played in groups. According to others, this grouping appeared only in the 16th century under the influence of commercial contacts with Islamic nations. In general, gong ensembles consist of gongs mounted on frames and instruments with metal tongues attached to a sound box (metallophones in Western terminology).

The Javanese gamelan

The most famous gong ensemble is the Javanese gamelan*. It is an orchestra including instruments with clearly defined functions. The first group is made up of instruments playing the basic melody (*balungan*). These are the *saron** or metallophones. The melody is also punctuated by separate gongs. The basic tune is varied by the *bonang** or horizontal gongs, the *gambang kayu** or xylophone, the *tjelempung* and the *siter*, a large and a small zither. A second melodic voice may be given to a rebab and a *suling* (flute) or perhaps to solo singers or a choir. Finally, there are the instruments giving the rhythm: these include mostly drums.

The tuning of these instruments is a real problem, as there is no standard. As well as this, the two musical systems used, *slendro* and *pelog*, are very

67. Gamelan, Java: *saron* **(metallophone),** *gambang* **(xylophone),** *bonang* **(set of gongs),** *ketjer* **(cymbals),** *kenong* **and** *ketuk* **(horizontal gongs),** *kempul* **and** *ageng* **(suspended gongs),** *kendang* **(drums)** (inv. M800 to M813, M823 & M824)

68. Gamelan of the Prince of Solo at the National Exhibition of Arnhem, 1879.
MIM, Brussels

different: they have only one note in common. *Slendro* has five notes for each octave, while *pelog* has seven. The pitch differs from one gamelan to another. The function of a gamelan orchestra is often religious. It accompanies the *wayang*, the puppet theatre which tells the Hindu epics of the Rāmāyana and the Mahābhārata. The best-known is the *wayang kulit*, the shadow puppet theatre. The gamelan is a part of all the rites of passage of the Javanese: birth, circumcision, purification, marriage, cremation and annual festivals, but is also played as a simple daily pastime.

37. Zithers in Africa and Asia

In the West, the zither was the starting point of keyboard instruments such as the harpsichord, the clavichord and the piano. A great variety of zithers are found in Asia, the Middle East and Africa. There are considerable differences in the way the instrument is played. Without any doubt, the oldest ones come from China.

The *qin** and the *se* apparently already existed in the 14th or 15th century B.C., under the Zhou dynasty (1122-221 B.C.). Charged with meaning and history, the *qin* is the symbol of erudition and knowledge. Its dimensions and the names of its different parts refer to cosmology and metaphysics. The dimensions symbolise the 365 days of the year, the curve of the case, the heavens and the bottom of the case, the earth. The *qin* has neither frets nor bridges and invariably has seven silk strings. It is an instrument for contemplation and art music. Under the Ming dynasty (1318-1644) there were twenty-four different styles of *qin*, each answering to a terminology inspired by philosophical considerations: 'pure', 'elegant', 'peaceful', etc.

69. *Qin* (zither), China (inv. M760)

The *koto* is the Japanese variation of the Chinese *se* and *zheng* (see no. 38). It is traditionally used for the accompaniment of singing and for *shirabemono* (purely instrumental music).

The present-day *shakuhachi* goes back to the itinerant Komusô monks of the 13th century. *Shakuhachi* music became very popular with Kurosawa Kinko (1710-1771), who left thirty-six pieces for the instrument. Since the 20th century, music written for the *koto* or *shamisen* has been performed on the *shakuhachi* or by the three instruments together.

In Kivu, as in Rwanda, the trough zither, generally more than a metre long, is the favourite accompaniment instrument of nomad singers. This instrument puts the listener into a trance. The *gombi* zither with its bark body is, on the contrary, used for relaxation. The *valiha** (Madagascar) and the *lotong* (Borneo) are typical examples of tube zithers.

The present-day *qanun*, a trapezoidal zither, seems to date from the 19th century. This board zither is found in the Arab world and Turkey, as well as in Greece (*kanonaki*). The name, as an indication of an instrument, does not

70. A Bara singer holding a *valiha*, Madagascar, c. 1900. Postcard.
MIM, Brussels

come from classical Arab lexicography. With a compass of three or four octaves, the number of strings was not fixed. In the 19th century this varied from sixty-six to seventy-five, and in Istanbul even reached eighty-one. The instrument is placed on the player's knees and is played with both hands. The tuning pins are on the left of the player. In 16th century Byzantine frescoes, the zither is often found in its trapezoidal form, held vertically. The *qanun*, which is probably a descendant, is now played essentially in bands.

38. Ritual music in Chinese temples

The groups of stone sticks (lithophones) and bronze bells are part of a long tradition. *Qing* (separate resonant stones) and *zhong* (bronze bells) already existed under the Shang dynasty (1766-1122 B.C.). *Bianqing* and *bianzhong*** (sets of stones or bells) go back to the Zhou dynasty (1122-221 B.C.). The examples found here date from the end of the 19th century.

71. *Bianzhong* **(set of bronze bells), Canton, China, c. 1900.** MIM, Brussels

The *bianqing* consists of a double row of sixteen suspended stones. Each stone measures 49cm by 33cm, but the thickness varies, thus allowing them to make different sounds. A *bianqing* is placed on the west side of each Confucian temple. The *bianzhong* has sixteen bells. This instrument is for both religious and court music. It is placed at the east side of the temple, so that the two instruments can dialogue.

Se and *zheng* are zithers made from hollow trunks of wood; in organological jargon they are called half-tube zithers. Normally, the *se* has twenty-five silk strings. The bridges can be moved, thus determining the tuning. After the Han dynasty (206 B.C.-220 A.D.), the *zheng* replaced the *se*. Under the Qing dynasty (1644-1911), many *se* were made in the old way; they are now to be found in museums. The modern *zheng* has metal strings. Ritual temple music also calls for several types of flute.

39. Ritual music in Tibetan monasteries

There is something fascinating in the music of the Tibetan monks. This may be because of the geographical situation of Tibet and its political isolation. The roof of the world is about 4,000 metres above sea-level. Since 1957 the spiritual head of the country, the Dalai Lama, has lived in exile in India. Tibetan Buddhist communities can obviously be found in India and Nepal, but are also found throughout the world.

The Tibetan monks use the *dung chen* (long trumpets) only for open-air ceremonies, where they dialogue with the *rgya gling** (oboe). The *dung chen* essentially come in two sizes: 170 to 180cm or 310cm. A few examples are even longer than four metres. The monks play long sounds linked by a sort of glissando.

The oboe players also use, as is frequently the case in Eastern countries, circular breathing (see no. 23). Other instruments, such as the *gandi* (woodblock), the *'khar rnga* (gong) and the *dung dkar* (conches) are used to summon the members of religious communities.

72. Monks playing the *rgya gling* (oboe), Zhe-chen monastery, Nepal, 1991.
© Mireille Helffer, Paris

73. *Rnga* (double-headed frame drum), Tibet (inv. 83.055/1)

To mark the time in a piece of music, the monks often use a *rnga** (frame drum) and three sorts of cymbals: *sbub-chal*, *sil nyan* and *ting shags*. Many drums are often used and it is not uncommon to meet with thirty or forty at the same time. Their role of giving a musical pulsation (cf. the metronome) is usually given to young monks.

Finally, there is a whole series of purely ritual objects like the *dril bu* and *gshang* (hand bells), the *damaru** (drum in the form of an hourglass) and the *rkang gling** or *rkang dung* (short trumpet made of human bone or metal). They are often represented as attributes of spiritual masters, divinities or even certain buddhas.

74. *Damaru* **(skull drum) and two** *rkang gling* **(femur trumpets), Tibet**
(inv. 4334, 4339 & 4340)

40. The oldest instruments

Small bells from Iran

Small openwork bells in the form of grenadines can be found in Luristan since the 9th century B.C. They have a magic function and are used to protect animals against evil spirits.

Egyptian instruments

The Egyptians adopted to their own aesthetic conceptions the form and sound of the instruments that they took from other sources. Thus we have a cat enthroned on a cittern and we find castanets in the form of a forearm.

Shoulder harps* existed for just one century under the 18th dynasty (1570-1320 B.C.). In addition, during this period, there was a fashion for banquet scenes showing groups including a harp, a lute and a double oboe, sometimes with a lyre and a frame drum as well.

The oboes were made from reeds from Greece: they date from either the Ptolemaic period (323-30 B.C.) or the Roman period (30 B.C.-395 A.D.).

75. A shoulder harp player. Detail of a wall painting of the tomb 241 of the Thebes necropolis, early 18th dynasty, c. 1500 B.C. The Supreme Council of Antiquities, Cairo; © Ingrid Leupen

Musical instruments on Grecian vases

Grecian vases (4th and 5th centuries B.C.) show lyre, *kithara* and *aulos** players in different combinations. A *kithara* is a large lyre with a wooden body. According to the legends, Hermes made the first lyre from the back of a tortoise. Nevertheless, representations of the lyre can be found in Mesopotamia from 2800 B.C. In Greece, the *kithara* was used to accompany singers, while the *aulos* (a double oboe) was used to accompany the choir.

76. A medaillon with red figures on a cup with an *aulos* player. Attributed to the Antiphon Painter, Attica, Greece, end of the archaic period, c. 480 B.C. (MRAH, Department of Antiquities, inv. R265)

These two musical genres both originated in the Dionysus cult, where percussion instruments such as drums and cymbals were added.

In their political essays, Plato and Aristotle banned the *kithara* and the *aulos* from their ideal city. This was not so much because of their horror of Dionisiac barbarianism but because the *kithara* was a virtuoso instrument and the tuning of the more recent *aulos* could be modified by finger technique. Thus these two instruments had moved away from the aristocratic tradition and had lost their educational interest. As well as this, for a long time there had been an ethical opposition between the lyre and the *aulos*. The lyre was considered to be the instrument of Apollo, the symbol of Grecian civilisation, while the *aulos* was the symbol of the barbarian Marsias.

41. Cantigas de Santa Maria

The *Cantigas de Santa Maria* is a collection of 420 songs composed and gathered together under the direction of Alfonso el Sabio (King Alphonse X the Wise), between 1260 and 1280. They are ballad-style songs, written in the vernacular, telling of the miracles performed by the Blessed Virgin. The songs are also famous because of the forty or so miniatures which illustrate and enhance them. The miniatures provide a glorious visual inventory of the instruments played in Spain in the Middle Ages, exceptional evidence which

77. Rebec players. A miniature taken from the *Cantigas de Santa Maria del Rey Alfonso el Sabio*, Spain, c. 1260-1280, f. 118r. Real Biblioteca de San Lorenzo, Escorial, Codex J.b.2; © Patrimonio nacional, Madrid

is made even more important by the fact that there are no surviving instruments of such an age.

The reign of Alphonse X the Wise was a short period of stability in the reconquest of a Spain which had been conquered by the Arabs in the 8th century. Christians, Arabs and Jews lived side by side, enjoying an exceptional wealth of culture. The *Cantigas* are written in the poetic style found to the north of the Pyrenees, but the illustrations show musicians with the clothes and skin colours of the three cultures. As for the instruments, some are undeniably European (bells, organ, hurdy-gurdy), others, of which there are a greater number, are Arabic (rebec*, lute, guitar, oboe, horn, bagpipe, percussion instruments, etc.). The variety is astonishing. The instruments were popularised by wandering minstrels and also by pilgrims returning from Compostella. They were to become the ancestors of some of the instruments which would soon be used all over Europe. At the end of the Middle Ages some of them disappeared, others were changed and developed. However, the authenticity of the evidence in the *Cantigas* is confirmed by the survival of comparable instruments in traditional cultures — both Arab and European.

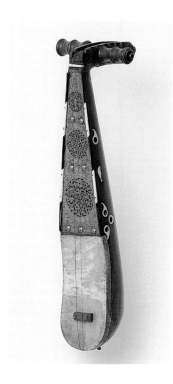

78. Rebab, Tunisia, 19th century
(inv. M378)

The rebab is the Arabic precursor of the European rebec of the Middle Ages.

The reliability of the illustrations

It would be tempting to see in the miniatures a true picture of the way in which the songs were accompanied. This is not the case. Although the scenes represented look authentic, it is more a case of illustrating an *instrumentarium* — a full catalogue of all the instruments used, than of a true representation. The way in which the instruments should be grouped remains a problem. On the other hand, the detail with which the instruments are illustrated makes the miniatures a gold mine of information.

The wealth of the instrumentarium of the Middle Ages

Almost forty different instruments can be seen in the *Cantigas*: five types of bowed strings, ten or so plucked stringed instruments, about fifteen wind instruments, five percussion instruments and an organ. They are usually shown in pairs of similar or related instruments. This is very much representative of one of the characteristics of the time — a huge wealth of variety. This is further reflected in their names, the full meaning of some of which has still not been discovered.

42. Minstrels in the 16th and 17th centuries

From the end of the 15th century, the use of musical instruments in towns and cities became much more common than before. All the minstrels, from the vagabond to the town musician with a fixed position, contributed greatly to this new situation. Until the end of the Middle Ages, the majority were still itinerant musicians. During the 16th century, many of these musicians settled in large cities,where, like other groups of artisans, they became associated in guilds. Guild regulations determined admission conditions, apprenticeship, working hours, competition, financial contributions and so on. In many

79. Detail from Jan I Brueghel, *A village wedding procession*, **Southern Low Countries, c. 1600.** © Museo del Prado – Madrid

Three violins accompany the bride to the church. These three instruments were usually of different sizes. An ensemble containing three to six violins was called a *bande* or *compagnie*. The smaller instruments were held on or against the shoulder. The larger ones were held by a strap around the neck. The bass was nearly in a horizontal position.

towns, minstrels could not perform alone nor in a group larger than six. A good minstrel had to be a good player of both wind and stringed instruments. In the first half of the 16th century, minstrels mostly used wind instruments, the most frequently used group consisting of three shawms (an ancestor of the oboe). From the mid-16th century on, five and six part music was often used, and dance music began to be played mostly on different-sized instruments of the violin family*. Nevertheless, for official ceremonies, wind instruments predominated for a long time. A typical wind group included three shawms*, a cornett* (a sort of small wooden trumpet), a dulcian* (precursor of the bassoon) and a sackbut* (trombone).

80. Town musicians. Detail from Denis Van Alsloot, *Ommegang of 1615 at Brussels.*
Procession in honour of Our Lady of the Sablon in Brussels on the 31st May.
© Museo del Prado – Madrid

This group of six musicians is based on two shawms and a bombarde (bass shawm). Groups
of three shawms have existed since the 15th century. New typically urban instruments
frequently joined this group in the second half of the 16th century: a cornett, a sackbut and a
dulcian.

Important towns officially employed five or six minstrels as town musicians.
Some minstrels were dancing masters, instrument makers or dealers.
Minstrels were called on for different festivities such as weddings and
banquets, and for public events such as receptions and processions. In
addition, from the end of the 16th century they regularly played in churches.

43. The Theatrum Instrumentorum of Michael Praetorius

This name is given to a volume of plates representing the musical instruments
of the time. Praetorius published it in 1620 in the second part of his *Syntagma*
Musicum. The instruments are drawn so finely and precisely to the scale of a
Brunswick foot (28.536cm) that we now know their exact measures.
The instruments are grouped into families and types. The principle of the
consort is fundamental to the ensemble music of the 16th and 17th centuries:
instruments are played either in families with a homogeneous timbre or in
groups with contrasting timbres. We notice especially the great diversity of
wind instrument families: recorders, transverse flutes, tabor pipes, shawms

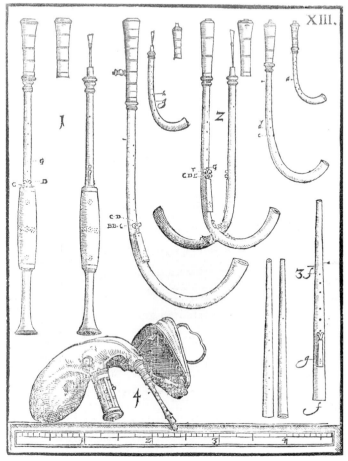

81. Small bass *corna musa* (no. 1), crumhorns (no. 2), straight cornetts (no. 3) and cornemuse (no. 4). Plate XIII of *Theatrum Instrumentorum* of Michael Praetorius, Wolfenbüttel, 1620. Engraving. MIM, Brussels

The *corna musa* is a straight crumhorn, which has a double reed enclosed in a cap.

and bombards, *bassanelli*, dulcians, *sordunen*, *cervelas*, crumhorns*, *kortholt*, *schryari*, cornetts, trumpets, trombones. The largest families, like the recorders and the shawms and bombards, have seven different-sized instruments. These highly-developed groups of instruments demonstrate the spirit of discovery and experimentation typical of the 16th century.

Praetorius' publication gives us the opportunity to make a better acquaintance with the viola da gamba*, which appeared at the beginning of the 16th century. Since this instrument fell into disuse toward the end of the Baroque period, it is often considered to be the forerunner of the violin. In fact, the gamba and the violin came into being almost simultaneously, notably as a result of the use of late types of fiddles and rebecs in several voices. This

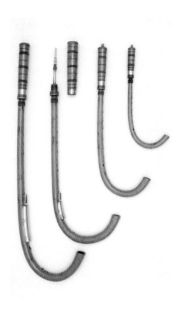

82. Crumhorn ensemble: soprano, tenor-alto, two basses. Italy?, second half of the 16th century
(inv. M615, M614, M611 & M610)

83. Alto viol, attributed to Heinrich Ebert, Venice, second half of the 16th century. Made up of parts cut from unknown origins (inv. M1402)

necessitated instruments of different sizes. To build and to play the larger instruments, the form had to be adapted. Thus the smaller instruments, often with three strings tuned in fifths, evolved in the direction of the violin, while the larger fiddles, with five or more strings, gave birth to the viola da gamba. The tuning of the gamba is based on the fourth and is almost always identical to that of the lute.

In the beginning, violinists usually played standing, with the larger instruments hanging from a neck-strap, whereas gambists played seated with the instrument either on the player's lap or between the legs. Thus the name *gamba* (leg). The sound is less forceful than that of the violin; perhaps this is the reason that the gamba was especially used for more refined music. Because of their size, the viols are fretted, making them easier to play in tune by amateurs, of which there were more and more in the 16th century. The bourgeoisie took the gamba to heart, and in the 17th century it was the preferred instrument of musical amateurs, who played polyphony with three to six viols, or with other instruments. The bass viol was also used to accompany new musical genres (lieder, sonatas, etc).

44. Stringed instrument making in Antwerp in the 16th and 17th centuries

Antwerp was world-famous for its harpsichords, but it was also a centre, in the 16th century, where citterns, lutes, viols and later violins were constructed with skill. Music had an important place among Antwerp's wealthy bourgeois. This is evident from the prosperity of its music printers and from the numerous musical subjects present in its paintings. In its role as a port city Antwerp exported musical instruments as well. A great number of lutes 'made in Flanders' appeared in early export documents.

Though builders of lutes and citterns made numerous instruments, most are now lost. Surviving Antwerp lutes can be counted on the fingers of one hand; none of the citterns preserved today can be attributed to the metropolis with certitude. Thus the little 1605 lute* signed by Matthijs Hofmans the Elder, the first known builder, is a rarity. Apparently it was saved by the decorative value of its ivory shell. The neck and peg-box are not from the original instrument.

The trade of violin maker (*luthier* in French, *violonsmaeker* in Dutch) is certified in documents dating from around 1650. Instruments related to the violin had already long been used in Antwerp's dance schools, but the musicians usually made them themselves. Around this time, Matthijs Hofmans (1622-1676) gave up lute making in favour of the violin. His instruments, with those of Hendrik Willems from Ghent, are considered the best from the Southern Low Countries. The violin dated 1665 and the dancing master's kit* are examples.

84. Soprano lute with case, Matthijs Hofmans the Elder, Antwerp, 1605 (inv. M1556)

85. Kit, Matthijs Hofmans, third quarter of the 17th century (inv. M2758)

The Hofmans family

The Hofmans family apparently left Germany for Antwerp in the second half of the 16th century. Two of its members, Jacques the Elder and Jacques the Younger, built lutes around 1600. Certain documents insinuate that Jacques the Younger led a dissipated life, but the lone survivor of his instruments shows his virtuosity in mastering the material. He was the great-uncle of Matthijs, a talented violin maker and until recently the only known practitioner of the trade in this family.

Archaic violin construction in the Southern Low Countries

As in other regions extending to the northern Alps (see no. 73), the Southern Low Countries long maintained an archaic building tradition in which the different pieces of the violin were first inserted into each other before gluing.

These instruments were thus not formed on a mould. The aesthetic characteristics of a series of 17th century Antwerp and Ghent instruments nonetheless betray Italian influence.

45. Harpsichord building in Antwerp in the 16th and 17th centuries

Historically, the importance of the Antwerp harpsichord building school is inestimable. From the 17th century their instruments, especially those of the Ruckers family, became so famous that they grew to be objects of transactions, adaptations and, for obvious financial reasons, large-scale counterfeits.

This building tradition can easily be followed from the middle of the 16th century because of the large number of surviving instruments and the documents in the archives. With the aim of safeguarding their professional interests, ten harpsichord builders obtained in 1558 the authorisation to become members of the Guild of Saint Luke. These ten builders were not required to produce a masterpiece, although this became an obligation for their successors. Among these ten builders were the Karest brothers. The MIM has a polygonal virginal from 1548 signed by Joannes Karest, an instrument bringing to mind both the Italian and the German traditions. The rectangular virginal by Joannes Grauwels*, from around 1580, ornamented by a grisaille painting in the style of Bruegel, is built in the famous Antwerp style. The original decoration of the outside of the case was rediscovered during a recent restoration.

The Ruckers family, the father Hans and his two sons Joannes and Andreas, made instruments richly ornamented with paintings as well as instruments with a simpler decoration in printed paper*. This style is immediately recognisable, with its seahorses and arabesques. Because of the high quality of their sound, many of these instruments were transformed, above all in France from the end of the 17th century. The aim of these transformations was to make the instruments adequate for playing the repertoire of the period. This technique of enlarging the instrument is called *ravalement*.

86. Lid of virginal, Joannes Grauwels, Antwerp, c. 1580
(inv. M2929). Painting restored thanks to the sponsorship of Fortis AG

87. *Muselaar* (rectangular virginal), Andreas Ruckers, Antwerp, **1620** (inv. M1597)

88. Detail of the rose and the soundboard of the Joannes Couchet harpsichord, Antwerp, **1646** (inv. M276)

A grandson of Hans, Joannes Couchet, perpetuated the tradition. His 1646 harpsichord* has two keyboards and four registers, giving the possibility of different sound colours. In the bass, there is the archaic short octave, i.e. the first bass octave does not have all the chromatic notes; although the keys of the first octave have the same appearance of those of the other octaves, some do not correspond to the same notes. The tradition of tempera painting of flowers, fruits and bird on the soundboard continued into the 18th century.

The Guild of Saint Luke

The Guild of Saint Luke was the name of the Antwerp painters' corporation. It is not surprising that the harpsichord builders preferred to belong to this guild rather than to that of the cabinetmakers. Effectively, the two trades had always been closely linked. Goossen Karest was a painter when he started his apprenticeship with his brother Joannes who was a harpsichord maker. Rubens himself decorated some Ruckers instruments.

46. Northern Italy

From the end of the Middle Ages, the ring of cities around the Alps played a dominant role in the development of instrumental music. Initially, the main activity was that of the musicians of Southern Germany, whereas in the 16th century, the itinerant and town musicians of Italy, especially in the regions from Milan to Venice, had more and more influence. Venice itself, thanks to its great period of political and economic stability and prosperity, attracted musicians and instrument builders from far and wide, becoming the most important musical centre of the time. The town of Füssen, on the Bavarian-Tyrol border, produced many luthiers, including the Kaiser family and the Sellas family. Many musicians, mainly violinists, came from Lombardy and the westernmost cities of the Venetian Republic. Some of them, like the Cicilianos and the Linarollos, were also stringed instrument makers.

Already in the first half of the 16th century, many important violinists resided in Brescia, and it became a centre of violin making. At the end of the 16th century, when the lute builders started to make violins, the Italian violin began to acquire its legendary stature. It was above all Cremona, a little town in the Po valley, that became renowned with makers such as the Amati family*, the Stradivarius family and Guarneri del Gesù.

In Europe generally, the violin was considered to be a vulgar instrument used principally for popular dances, whereas in Northern Italy it was used very early for serious music. Even before the mid-16th century, it was being played in churches, often with the organ. It was also used for serious music outside of a religious context more often than in other regions. From Italy comes the baroque repertoire of concertos and sonatas, which was developed by composers like Corelli and Vivaldi.

89. Violin, attributed to Antonio and Girolamo Amati, Cremona, 1611
(inv. 4160)

90. *Chitarrone*, **Matteo (I) Sellas (Seelos), Venice, first half of the 17th century** (inv. M255)

91. Cornett, Bassano family, Venice, third quarter of the 16th century (inv. M1202)

The harmonic underlay of this new music, called basso continuo, was played on large lutes called theorbos or *chitarrone*. They were often used with the harpsichord.

Theorbo and chitarrone

The theorbo, also called *chitarrone** by the Italians until the middle of the 17th century, is a large lute which has long bass strings in addition to the melody strings. Rarely played solo, it was used in a continuo group, or to accompany vocal music. Its music was notated in tablature, a system based on the position of the fingers on the strings.

The cornett

At the end of the 16th and throughout the 17th century the high parts of the violin repertoire were often played by cornetts*. Sometimes it was played in alternation with the violin, and sometimes for accompanying vocal lines. The instrument resembles a wooden horn with finger holes. It is usually curved and made from two pieces of leather-covered wood with a trumpet-like embouchure.

47. French 17th and 18th century court music

The Sun King, Louis XIV, himself on stage dancing the role of the Sun God, is a cogent illustration of the significance of dance and music at the very top of the European political pyramid. The French court had created three institutions which, since the mid-16th century, worked to increase the influence of French culture throughout Europe and further afield. These were the *Chapelle*, the *Chambre*, and the *Écurie*. Upon the *Chambre* depended the king's gambists, lutenists and his famous 24 Violins. The *Écurie* had five groups of musicians, mainly wind instruments, but also strings. The trumpet marine and the 12 violinists played with crumhorns, oboes, sackbuts and cornetts. Towards the end of the 17th century, the *Écurie* slowly became two

92. Engraving by Nicolas Dupuis after Charles Dulin, *The Twelve Large Oboes of the Grande Écurie***. Detail of the** *Royal Feast***, plate IX of the** *Crowning of Louis XV at Rheims on October 25, 1722***, Paris, 1722.** © The French National Library, Paris

93. *Musette de cour*, **Chédeville, Paris, 18th century** (inv. M1125)

groups: one of trumpets and one of oboes*. These ensembles were used outdoors for parades, for welcoming ambassadors, the return from the hunt, religious ceremonies, etc.

The Hotteterre family provided several generations of players and instrument builders to the *Grande Écurie*. Coming from the town of La Couture-Boussey in Normandy, they inherited a century-old tradition of woodworking. They are recognised as being instrumental in the transformation of woodwind instruments: recorders, transverse flutes, oboes, bassoons, flageolets and musettes. Originally built from a single piece of wood, they were now in sections.

The musette* is a kind of bagpipe, and, entering the musical life of the court at the same time as the hurdy-gurdy, it acquired new prestige. The Chédeville family as well as the Hotteterres built musettes.

48. French viols in the 17th and 18th centuries

At the end of the 17th century, France was one of the last countries where the viola da gamba was still widely used, as much by amateurs as by court professionals. This can be explained notably by the amateurs' contemptuous attitude toward the violin, associated with dance music and itinerant minstrels held in low esteem. Bourgeois and aristocrats, fascinated with court life, were more segregated in France than amateurs in other countries where the violin had long been an accepted diversion.

This attitude was to cause problems, above all at a time when Italian violin music was growing more and more popular in France. To be able to play this often virtuoso repertoire on the gamba, existing viols began to be adapted so

94. Bass viol, Romain Chéron, Paris, c. 1700 (inv. M1432)

95. *Quinton* (high treble viol), Louis Guersan, Paris, 1753 (inv. M1394)

that bourgeois and chamber musicians could continue to avoid the violin and the violoncello. A seventh string, tuned lower, was often added to the bass viol*, an addition made possible by overwound strings with greater mass. Composers like Marin Marais, Saint-Colombe and Antoine Forqueray wrote extravagant music for this type of viol.

Besides bass viols, the French increasingly used smaller viols, not in consort but for solos which closely resembled violin music. During the 18th century they even played true violin music, a reason for reducing the size of the venerable *dessus de viole* (treble viol) to create the *pardessus de viole* (high treble viol), tuned a fourth higher. The latter became in turn the *quinton**, a hybrid instrument with many of the violin's features. The *quinton* has only five strings and is partially tuned in fifths. The latest types of *quintons* could be held on the knees like a gamba or under the chin like a violin, and closely resembled violins.

The relation between viol and violin in French treatises

1706 - Lecerf de la Viéville, *Comparaison de la Musique Italienne et de la Musique Françoise*: 'The Violin is not noble in France, we are all agreed. That is, one no longer sees people of quality who play it, but many low musicians who make their living with it'.

1740 - Hubert Le Blanc, *Defense de la Basse de Viole contre les Entreprises du violon et les Pretentions du violoncelle*: 'Sultan Violin, an Abortion, a Pygmy, took it into his head to run the universal Monarchy. Not content with his share of Italy, he proposes to invade the neighbouring States'.

1756 - Diderot and d'Alembert, *Encyclopédie*, on viols: 'they are tuned here by fourths, there by fifths, just like violins, at the will of the musician'.

1757 - Ancelet, *Observations sur la Musique, les musiciens et les instruments*: 'The violin is becoming more and more fashionable, and people of quality may now play it'.

49. The Brussels court

In the 17th century, the court chapel, having become a permanent part of court life, received its own administrative structure. The members of the *cappella* played for religious services, while the *camera* performed secular music. For important occasions, these groups were reinforced by local or sometimes foreign musicians. The existing receipt books relating to these musicians reflect the evolution of the chapel. There were a series of singers, an organist and a group of instrument players which continuously grew, although the total number of musicians varied with the economic context.

The circle of musicians and instrument makers formed a small group. Members of the Borbon, Snoeck and Rottenburgh families can be found in both groups for several generations. In the mid-17th century, instrument repairs were still very badly paid, but this was to improve in the 18th century, when the builders were held in somewhat better regard. One can conclude, looking at the conserved stringed instruments, that these were of good quality. The accounts also indicate instruments delivered to the court. The chapel had some Italian violins. The growing importance of wind instruments in the 18th century orchestra can be seen at the court. In 1772, François-Guillaume Rottenburgh was employed as 'luthier for wind instruments'. Ten years later the decline in musical life was under way and the court chapel was dissolved with the French Revolution.

96. Kit, Gaspar Borbon, Brussels, 1686
(inv. M2764)

97. Alto recorder, transverse flute, oboe, Jean-Hyacinthe (I or II) Rottenburgh; clarinet and clarinet *d'amore*, Godefroid-Adrien Rottenburgh, Brussels, second and third quarters of the 18th century
(inv. M1027, M1077, M2608, M915 & M2595)

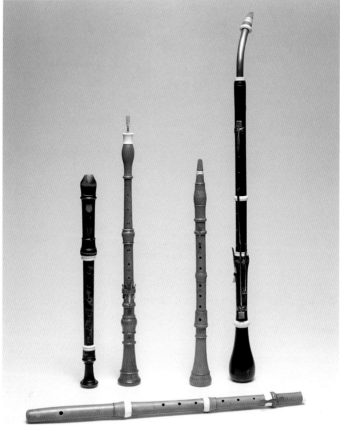

98. Tenor violin, Gaspar Borbon, Brussels, 1692 (inv. M2836)

99. Violoncello, Marcus Snoeck, Brussels, 1718 (inv. M1373)

Gaspar Borbon (c. 1635-1710)

As well as his violas da gamba, Gaspar Borbon above all made instruments of the violin family, from the dancing master's kit* to the large violoncello. From at least 1664 Borbon was the court luthier. According to the tradition of the Southern Low Countries, his instruments were constructed without a mould or form. This archaic technique was still used in these regions until the middle of the 18th century.

The Rottenburgh family

At the court, several members of this family rose to the rank of first or second violin, although the family is known above all for their woodwind making*. The quality of their instruments was so high that counterfeits of their instruments were known even during their lifetime.

Charles de Lorraine

Under the regency of Charles de Lorraine in the Southern Low Countries (1749-1780), the Brussels court chapel attained a very high level. It should be noted that the devotion and the talent of the Kapellmeister and composer Henri-Jacques De Croes greatly contributed to this flowering.

50. Nuremberg

Brass instruments

From the 16th to the 19th century Nuremberg was an important centre of wind instrument making. During this long period, sixty-two brass instrument makers were working there, exporting to all the known world. The Ehe, Haas and Hainlein families made instruments for the imperial court, the Elector of Brandenburg, the Archbishop of Salzburg, the King of Poland, Duke Karl Theodor of the Palatinate and the Archbishop of Bamberg. Nuremberg trumpets are mentioned in the archives of Bamberg and Graz as well as in those of the Wurtemberg court and those of the town of Nuremberg.

From 1625, the trumpet*, horn and trombone makers of Nuremberg formed a guild with strict rules, the object of which was to forbid trade secrets to be divulged to people outside the town. The guild also chose a sort of trademark, in this case an eagle. Even the use of trumpets was restricted. Only selected musicians could play it, because trumpets were instruments which called people to action, instruments which could be given only to people worthy of this responsibility.

Christoph Weigel, Der Trompetenmacher

In his Nuremberg workshop, the trumpet maker is working at the showpiece of a brass instrument: the bell. Making the bell on the anvil is the most difficult part of this work and that which requires the greatest know-how. The tools shown in this engraving* allow us to follow the different stages in the manufacture of the instrument.
- Knives and pincers (A) are used to cut different pieces to the required shape: two pieces cut and partially made can be seen on the table (B).
- After the initial cutting, the piece of metal is hammered on an anvil (C), first with wooden, then with metal hammers (D).
- The body of the instrument is then assembled: teeth cut along the edges are assembled and soldered; the solder joint is hammered on the anvil.
- Different forms (E) are available for making the bell.
- The joint is then pulled into shape on the bench, then smoothed with the plane (F) and polished.
- The placing of a reinforcing crown at the end of the bell, as well as making large bells, requires the use of a U-form (G).

100. Christoph Weigel, *Der Trompetenmacher*. Engraving from *Ständebuch. Abbildung der Gemein-Nützlichen Haupt-Stände... biß auf alle Künstler u. Handwerker*, Regensburg, 1698. Bayerische Staatsbibliothek, Munich

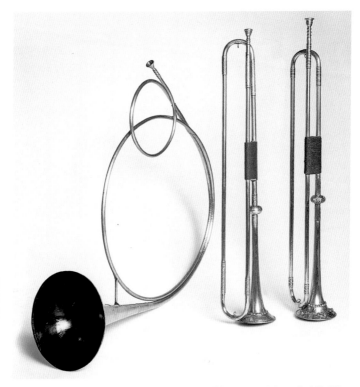

101. Horn, Johann Leonard (II) Ehe, Nuremberg, 1709; trumpet, Johann Carl Kodish, Nuremberg, 1693; trumpet, Johann Leonard (II) Ehe, Nuremberg, 1690-1724 (inv. M3152, M1176 & M1177)

Woodwinds

In Nuremberg, five different makers had the name of Denner: the most important were Johann Christoph Denner* (1655-1707) and his son Jakob Denner (1681-1735). Johann Christoph Denner was one of the first makers outside of France who was to assimilate the improvements of Hotteterre; this is shown by a request addressed with Johann Schell to the municipal council of Nuremberg in 1696. Denner and Schell asked to be admitted into the guild of makers of decoys and horns, or at least to be recognised as 'free masters'. There was then no flutemakers' guild. Denner and Schell added to their request that they made oboes and *flaudadois* (the French *flûte douce*, a type of recorder) 'which were invented in France about twelve years ago', and which 'on our good faith, are now made at Nuremberg for the first time'.

The 'invention' of the clarinet

The name of Johann Christoph Denner has long been associated with the invention of the clarinet*. This assertion goes back to an article by J.G.

Doppelmayr in his *Historische Nachricht von den Nürenbergischen Mathematicis und Künstlern* (Nuremberg, 1730). The article on Johann Christoph Denner says that he invented the clarinet and perfected the *chalumeau*. Like the clarinet, the *chalumeau* is a single-reed instrument, but distinguished from the clarinet by the impossibility of playing an octave higher. This characteristic keeps the *chalumeau* in a limited register.

However, it is not altogether clear that Johann Christoph Denner was really the inventor of the clarinet; it is even questioned that he ever made any clarinets. The first orders for clarinets were made after his death and concern his son, Jacob. Be this as it may, as many clarinets as *chalumeaux* signed Denner are now conserved. At Nuremberg, only the Denners made *chalumeaux*, while other clarinet makers, such as Johann Wilhelm I Oberländer (1681-1763) and his son Johann Wilhelm II (1712-1779) were also working there. Three Oberländer clarinets with two keys have been conserved.

Christoph Weigel, Der Pfeiffenmacher

It is quite plausible that Johann Christoph Denner is shown on this engraving titled 'The Chalumeau Maker'*. Amongst the production of this artisan are found a majority of double-reed instruments: *chalumeaux* and bombardes (nos. 1, 2), a eunuch flute (no. 3), a bassoon (no. 4), a *Chorist-Fagott* (no. 5), but also instruments with a mouthpiece such as cornetts (no. 6) or instruments of the recorder family: a tenor recorder (no. 7) and a tuning flute (no. 8). The maker in the illustration is working on a bassoon. The tools shown allow us to bring to mind the characteristic stages of building any woodwind instrument.

- The piece of wood is given its approximate dimensions with an axe (A).
- The form is made on a lathe, using different chisels (B).
- The interior is hollowed with gouges (C).
- The finger-holes are made by drills (D).
- Possible extra pieces such as keys are added (E).

51. The orchestra of Johann Sebastian Bach

Between 1723 and 1750 Johann Sebastian Bach was Kapellmeister at the *Thomaskirche* in Leipzig. The orchestra at his disposal was not a fixed group, but comprised a mixture of professionals and amateurs. The nature and the number of the performers was continuously changing. During the period of Bach's predecessor, Johann Kuhnau, the professional town musicians, the *Stadtpfeifer* (winds) and the *Kunstgeiger* (strings), came together in one body, the *coro primo*, for the performance of the Sunday cantata at the *Thomaskirche*. The amateur musicians were graduates or students at the university.

The main difference between the four *Stadtpfeifer* and the three *Kunstgeiger* was in social status: the *Kunstgeiger* had a lower status and were paid less.

102. Christoph Weigel, *Der Pfeiffenmacher*. **Engraving from** *Ständebuch. Abbildung der Gemein-Nützlichen Haupt-Stände... biß auf alle Künstler u. Handwerker*, **Regensburg, 1698.** Bayerische Staatsbibliothek, Munich

The *Stadtpfeifer* also played stringed instruments, while the *Kunstgeiger* slowly started learning to play wind instruments. At first, the primary obligations of the *Stadtpfeifer* were to play fanfares twice every day on the steps of the town hall. In Bach's period, their instruments included the trumpet, cornett, oboe and trombone.

103. Clarinet in C, Denner, Nuremberg, first third of the 18th century (inv. M912)

104. Elias Gottlaub Haußmann, *Gottfried Reiche*, **Leipzig, 1727. Engraving.**
© Museum für Geschichte der Stadt Leipzig

One should not be surprised by the variety presented in Bach's cantatas and passions, especially as regards wind instruments. Bach wrote solos for trumpet, slide trumpet (*tromba da tirarsi*), cornett, trombone, chromatic horn, hunting horn, recorder, traverse flute, oboe, *oboe da caccia*, *oboe d'amore* and bassoon. As for the strings, we find a few solos for unusual instruments such as the *violino piccolo*, the *violetta*, the *viola d'amore*, the *viola da gamba* as well as the violoncello.

The permanent musicians that Bach could use at Leipzig are known by name. Without any doubt, the most famous was Gottfried Reiche*, immortalised with his trumpet in a painting. For him, Bach wrote his most virtuoso solos, notably the second Brandenburg Concerto and the B Minor Mass. Reiche died on 6 October 1734 at the age of sixty-seven, the day after performing, before the Elector of Saxony, the extremely difficult trumpet solo from the dedicatory cantata *Preise dein Glücke, gesegnetes Sachsen* (BWV 215).

105. *Viola d'amore*, **Johannes Rauch, Komotau, Bohemia, Czech Republic, 1742** (inv. M1391)

The viola d'amore

The *viola d'amore** is a hybrid instrument known since the end of the 17th century, especially in the south-east of the German-speaking region of Europe. It is characterised by a variable number of sympathetic metal strings, vibrating by resonance, placed under the played gut strings. The body is comparable to that of a small viol. The sympathetic strings pass through a hollow and relatively long neck. The number of strings as well as the tuning can be quite varied. The *viola d'amore* is played on the shoulder, very much like the violin. Its repertoire consists mainly of solo pieces, but Bach used it to accompany solo arias.

106. Georg Balthasar Probst, *Hearing*, **Augsburg, c. 1765. Engraving.**
Photo MIM, Brussels

The performance of a cantata in a town building. This engraving was pierced with holes for using for optical viewing with backlighting.

52. Potsdam

It was at Potsdam that Johann Joachim Quantz (1697-1773) taught Frederick the Great of Prussia how to play the flute*. As well as this, Quantz contributed to the development of the instrument and composed about three hundred concertos for the flute. His treatise on the transverse flute, *Versuch einer Anweisung die Flöte traversiere zu spielen*, was so successful that it was translated into Dutch in 1752. As for the organological evolution of the transverse flute, Quantz is known above all for the introduction of the second key. In this period the corps de rechange (different joints for playing at different pitches) were introduced. These enabled performers to play in tune at different pitches. Frederick the Great owned such a flute made in ivory by Scherer* of Butzbach.

107. Peter Haas, *Concert at the château of Sans Souci near to Potsdam, with Frederick the Great playing solo flute,* **Berlin?, c. 1775. Engraving.**
© Royal College of Music, London, Department of Portraits

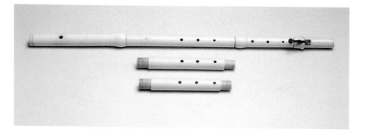

108. Transverse flute in ivory with two corps de rechange, Johannes Scherer, Butzbach, Germany, 18th century (inv. M448)

53. Haydn and Eszterháza

The baryton* was the favourite instrument of Prince Nikolaus Esterházy, Joseph Haydn's protector for thirty years. Like the *viola d'amore*, the baryton, underneath the gut strings, had a variable number of metal strings which sounded by sympathetic resonance. Like the viol, it was held between the knees. The back of the relatively large neck was open, so that the sympathetic strings could also be plucked by the thumb. This gave the baryton musical possibilities close to those of the lute. Around 1600, the English viol players apparently already used sympathetic strings on their instruments, with the aim of approaching the sound of the lute. During the 17th century, sympathetic strings also came to be appreciated in Germany. At the end of the century, the *viola d'amore* and the baryton became popular in Southwestern Germany, Austria and Bohemia. All the authors describing these instruments say that they are charmed by the 'pleasant and harmonious'

sound of the baryton. Haydn wrote more than a hundred trios for the baryton.

Haydn also composed a great deal for keyboard instruments. As well as the clavichord and the pianoforte, he also used the harpsichord. He owned a harpsichord offered by the London makers Burkat Shudi and John Broadwood. His harpsichord was practically identical to that of the MIM*, made in 1773 as a gift of Frederick the Great to Maria Theresa of Austria. Its features include two pedals, one operating a 'Venetian swell' (like a Venetian blind placed over the soundboard, allowing a certain control over the dynamics). The other pedal, known as the machine stop, changed the registers used while leaving the hands free. The aim of such inventions was to help the 'inexpressive' harpsichord compete with the new pianoforte, which offered more expressive possibilities.

109. Baryton, anonymous, Southern Germany or Austria, early 18th century (inv. M231)

110. Harpsichord, Burkat Shudi & John Broadwood, London, 1773 (inv. M1604)

Leopold Mozart on the baryton (Versuch einer gründlichen Violinschule, Augsburg, 1756):

The tenth kind is the Bordon, from the Italian Viola di Bordone. This instrument has, like the gamba, six to seven strings. It has a very wide neck, the back side of which is hollow and open and into which nine or ten brass and steel strings are inserted, which are touched and plucked by the thumb. Moreover, while the principal part is played by the bow on the gut strings, the thumb simultaneously plucks the bass part on the strings under the neck. Consequently, compositions have to be written specially for it. It is, however, one of the most charming of instruments.

54. Music for wind bands at the time of Mozart

During the second half of the 18th century, music for wind bands was especially appreciated by the aristocracy of Central Europe. This is entertaining music for wind instruments, the most frequent orchestration being for two clarinets, two oboes, two horns and two bassoons. The band of Prince Schwarzenberg in the 1770s included two oboes, two english horns, two horns and two bassoons. Even the Emperor Joseph II created an Imperial Band in 1783. As ever, the bourgeois circles imitated the nobility and quickly

111. The band of the Prince of Œttingen-Wallerstein, Harburg, 1791. Silhouettes.
Fürst Wallerstein Schlösser und Museen Harburg

adopted this type of music. The *Wiener Theater-Almanach* of 1794 relates: 'During the summer months, nearly every day, when the weather allows it, small groups can be seen in the streets. This can be at any time, and sometimes very late... This evening music is given by wind quartets, quintets, sextets and sometimes complete orchestras'. The influence of the French Masonic lodges in the formation of these bands should be noted. In Paris there were no less than seven bands in the lodges at the end of the 18th century. The orchestra of Œttingen-Wallerstein* was a typical band of the period. Active between 1745 and 1812, its peak was between 1780 and 1792. The music for these groups was often written by great composers. The Œttingen-Wallerstein band played music by F.A. Hoffmeister, Mozart, Ignace Pleyel, Antonin Reicha and Antonio Rosetti. Haydn wrote some *Feldpartien* from 1759 for the Count Maximilian Morzin, just as Mozart composed his *Tafelmusik* for wind instruments for the Archbishop of Salzburg. Along with these original works for a wind band, there are countless arrangements. In France, what was called a *pièce d'harmonie* ('music for a wind band') generally consists of about six pieces, usually short extracts taken from operas. Transcriptions were also very popular in Central Europe. In a letter to his father dated 20 July 1782, Mozart wrote that he was working on a transcription of the opera *Die Entführung aus dem Serail* for a wind band. Johann Nepomuk Went (1745-1801) and Joseph Triebensee (1772-1846) were both important arrangers working for the Imperial Band.

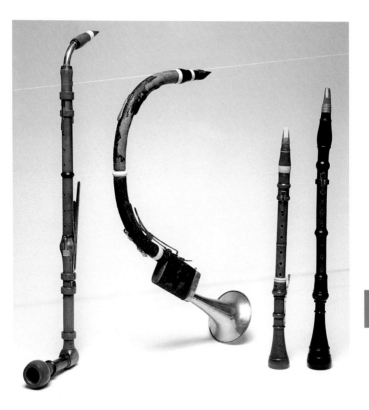

112. Two basset horns, anonymous, Germany, 18th century; clarinet, Johannes
Scherer, Butzbach, Germany, 18th century; B flat clarinet, Jean-Baptiste Willems,
Bruxelles, second half of the 17th century - beginning of the 18th century
(inv. M934, M935, M924 & M2573)

55. The influence of Turkish music

Europe hesitated a long time between fascination and aversion for Eastern
music. Arabs and Turks were considered as pagans menacing the Christian
West. This is doubtless the reason why percussion instruments, so present in
Turkish and Arabic music, were banned for a long time in Europe. Here, only
army bands and their folk music equivalents had integrated percussion
instruments: timpani were associated with trumpets, drums with flutes.

At the end of the 17th century and during the 18th century the Turks were no
longer considered to be a political menace. Thanks to their exotic character,
they were shown at the theatre and the opera. Their appearance on the stage
was accompanied by 'Turkish' percussions: bass drums, Turkish crescents*,
bells, triangles and cymbals.

The imagination of the period concerned itself with Turkish military music.
Effectively, the Turkish armies of the period had important bands of
musicians, called Janissary bands. From the beginning of the 18th century,

113. Turkish crescent, attributed to Charles-Joseph Sax, Paris, first half of the 19th century (inv. M881)

after the decline of the Ottoman Empire, the sultans offered companies of Janissaries to the monarchs of Central Europe. In Vienna, such companies were very fashionable around 1750, and about 1770 nearly all the armies in Europe had their own Janissaries. Turkish marches became so popular that, at the beginning of the 19th century, Viennese pianos often had a 'Turkish' pedal which played a percussion group consisting of bells, a drum and an imitation of cymbals. In French regiments, black Africans rather than Turks played the percussion instruments*. As well as the Turkish instruments, they also used tambourines. This is why the percussion pedal of French pianos also has a tambourine stop.

In parallel with the percussion instruments, the military bands were enlarged with new wind instruments. The most important new instrument was the serpent, a sinuous wooden instrument covered with leather, used from the 16th century in churches. Serpents were used for the bass part, for which there was not yet any other military wind instrument.

From the end of the 18th century, janissary instruments appeared in orchestral music. The evolution clearly shows that composers such as Haydn and Mozart still clearly associated this type of instrument with oriental and military music. After Beethoven, however, the janissary instruments, along with the timpani, formed the basis of the percussion section of the romantic orchestra. The serpent kept its place in the orchestra during the first decades of the 19th century until it was supplanted by the bass tuba.

Charles Burney on the subject of military music in Lille (The Present State of Music in Germany and the Low Countries, London, 1773):

To persons who stay but a short time in French garrisoned towns, military parade affords considerable amusement; there are, at present, only four battalions, or two thousand men, quartered in the city; though it is usual for the garrison to consist of ten thousand. The mounting guard upon the *Grande Place*, or square, is, in itself, a gay and entertaining sight; yet it always gives me a melancholy, and painful sensation, to see the people outnumbered by the

114. Charles Vernier, *Costumes de l'armée française. Musiciens*, Paris, c. 1845. Engraving. MIM, Brussels

The contact with Turkish culture was more direct in Central Europe than in France, where Turkish instruments entered into use only after the French Revolution. The new percussion instruments were first played by Africans, then by men with a blackened face.

military... Having visited this city, in quest of musical information, so lately as the year 1770, I expected to find nothing new, that was very interesting; however, I attended to the military music, which is much changed here since I was last in France. The marches, as well as musicians, are chiefly German. The *crotolo* is used here as I had seen it at Florence; it serves very well to mark the time in marching, though it has only one tone, like that of a side drum: it is the same instrument as that which the ancients called the *cymbalum*. The Turks were the first among the moderns who used it in their troops; the form is that of a bason, or the cover to a dish; there is one for each hand. It is made of brass, but the vibration is so stopt by its being in contact with the hand, that it cannot be called sonorous, it is rather a clashing than a sounding instrument of percussion; however, its effect in marking the time is so powerful as to be distinctly heard through the stunning noise of forty drums.

56. La banda at the opera

All the instruments conceived by Sax, including the saxophone, were used in the opera, both on stage and in the orchestra. From 1847, the brass section of the Paris opera was placed under the direction of Adolphe Sax himself. It played in nearly all the important operas to be staged there between 1847 and 1894, with the exception of the comic operas. Giacomo Meyerbeer used the banda in his great operas, as did Charles Gounod, Giuseppe Verdi, Ambroise

115. Adolphe Sax's saxhorns with six independent valves and a rotating bell: alto in E flat, Paris, 1863; bass in B flat, Paris, 1867; contrabass in E flat, Paris, 1867; contrabass in B flat, Paris, 1867 (inv. M2469, M2464, M2460 & M1283)

Thomas and Jules Massenet. The saxtuba made a spectacular entrance in Fromenthal Halévy's *Le Juif errant* in 1852. In 1867 Adolphe Sax invented the 'new saxhorns', or saxhorns with six independent valves* and used them for the famous autodafé scene in Verdi's opera *Don Carlos*, in Paris. In 1871, Sax used a whole series of trumpets for the renowned trumpet march in the Paris production of *Aïda*.

In Brussels Mahillon's firm made brass instruments for the Théâtre de la Monnaie, in particular Wagner tubas and a bass trumpet for the *Ring des Nibelungen* by Richard Wagner.

57. Basso profundo

By the end of the 18th century wind bands were growing in size and it became clear that new instruments were needed to strengthen the lower registers. The bassoon and the serpent had relatively weak sounds and could not compete with the growing numbers of clarinets, bugles, cornets, horns and trombones.

To begin with, instrument makers tried to modernise the serpent in order to create a bass instrument. This gave rise to the Russian bassoon, the serpent-bassoon, the military serpent, the Forveille bassoon* and the metal ophicleide. When the use of pistons began to spread between 1815 and 1830, they were gradually added to the bass brass instruments and in particular to the ophicleides*. These new instruments were known in France and Belgium as *basses d'harmonie*, and as *Wiener Bombardon* in Germanic countries. They were also made in Belgium by such makers as Georg Christian Bachmann and Charles Mahillon.

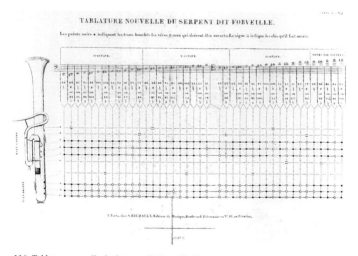

116. *Tablature nouvelle du Serpent dit Forveille.* **Extract from an anonymous tutor for the serpent, Paris, beginning of the 19th century.** MIM, Brussels

**117. Monster ophicleide in E flat,
France?, c. 1830** (inv. 1248)

**118. Bass tuba in F, Carl Wilhelm Moritz
and Wilhelm Friedrich Wieprecht, Berlin,
c. 1840** (inv. M1281)

The bass tuba* of Carl Wilhelm Moritz and Wilhelm Wieprecht (Berlin, 1835) is considered to be one of the first fully fledged valved bass instruments, although the German military bands continued to use the trombone as a bass voice for quite some time.

Adolphe Sax also made his contribution to the question of the lower registers. When he was developing his families of saxhorns, saxotrombas and saxtubas in the 1840s he was concerned with the problem of covering the whole range of registers, from the very highest to the lowest. He was therefore aware of the bass and double bass register. The appearance of the *saxhorn bourdon* in the Paris World Fair in 1855 created a sensation and gave rise to numerous cartoons.

In the second half of the 19th century preference was given to bugle-type instruments, in other words to conical brass instruments such as the bombardon, the tuba, or the sousaphone. From now on it would be these instruments which would provide the deepest register amongst the brass instruments. There was one other addition — the brass double bassoon, which had a variety of names — the *Universal double bassoon* or *Tritonikon*, *contrabasse à anche*, or *contrabass sarrusophone*.

58. The instruments of Adolphe Sax

Adolphe Sax (1814-1894) was not the only instrument maker to give his name to a musical instrument. Many inventors of the 19th century used their names for their inventions; for example the sarrusophone, the antoniophone, the sudrophone, the rothphone, the müllerphone and the heckelphone. The saxophone family is the best known of the four families of musical instruments developed by Sax. The other three families — saxhorns, saxotrombas*, and saxtubas have an identical mouthpiece to the horn or the bugle, whereas the saxophones have a single reed.

Invented around 1840, the saxophone* had not only an original design, but also a new key system. All the instruments in the family can be played with the same fingering and all the music can be read in the G clef. In addition, saxophones are relatively easy to play, easy to hold and are capable of a great range of expression. Sax developed them as an alternative to stringed instruments for use in outdoor ensembles, but they blend harmoniously into an orchestra.

119. Trombone in E flat in the form of a saxotromba, Adolphe Sax, Paris 1866; contrabass saxhorn in B flat with three pistons, Adolphe Sax, Paris, 1854 (inv. M3284 & M2459)

**120. Adolphe Sax saxophones: soprano,
Paris, 1860; alto, Paris, 1862; tenor,
Paris, 1860; baritone, Paris, 1860**
(inv. M3111, JT207, 3765 & 3663)

121. View of a part of the ground floor workshop. Detail of *Manufacture d'instruments de musique de M. Sax, rue Saint-Georges, Paris. World Exhibition, London 1862.* Extract from *Le Monde Illustré*, Paris 1863

The warehouse that Sax rented from the flautist Dorus still exists today. From 1842 until the third bankruptcy of Sax in 1877, the building housed several workshops and an exhibition and concert hall. Today it is used for shops and apartments.

Sax is an important figure not only because of the originality of his inventions, but also because of the influence both he and his instruments had on the development of French military bands and on Parisian musical life in general. The military bands of Germany and Austria were characterised by the bright, brassy sounds of the trumpets and trombones. The Sax instruments however, offered new, far more mellow sounds and the French gradually replaced the bugle with the saxhorn and the horn with the saxotromba in the middle registers. The orchestral palette was thus radically changed.

59. The Belgian clarinet

The French were the first to apply the innovations of Theobald Boehm to the clarinet. The new instrument, called the 'Boehm clarinet' had a system of keys which could open and close the furthest holes. In this way it was possible to achieve a greater chromatic range. The Boehm clarinet was developed between 1839 and 1843 and was the result of a collaboration between Louis-Auguste Buffet, a French wind instrument maker, and the clarinettist Hyacinthe Éléonore Klosé. Its popularity spread rapidly throughout France.

The Belgians, however, were highly dubious of this type of clarinet. They were using the old model with thirteen keys that they had developed into a light, easy-to-play, quality instrument, which was capable of playing in tune.

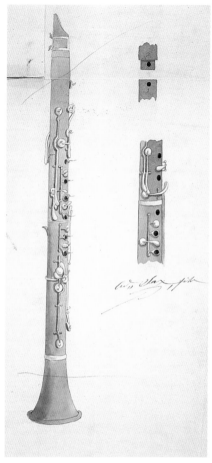

122. Drawing of a clarinet attached to the patent application no. 1326/2244 in the name of Adolphe Sax junior, Brussels, 27 May 1842.
Ministry of Economic affairs, Brussels

123. Clarinet in B flat, Victor-Charles Mahillon, Brussels, 1867 (inv. M2300)

In 1840 and 1842, Adolphe Sax, himself a good clarinettist, patented two ring key systems for the clarinet*, but despite all expectations he never actually made such an instrument. The bass clarinet that he patented in 1839 was another project. It was to be another fifteen years or so before the instrument makers Albert and Mahillon would rediscover the key system of Sax and apply it to the clarinet. The 'Albert clarinet' had ring keys on the lower joint, and occasionally on the upper joint as well.

The Albert clarinet was a great success and was manufactured cheaply to compete with the Boehm clarinet. It was popular with jazzmen, including Benny Goodman, until the Second World War.

60. The industrialisation of instrument making

Contrary to popular belief, industrialisation has never replaced the craftsman in instrument making. Even if it affected certain sectors in a dramatic way, most workshops remained medium-sized or small. In those areas where industrialisation did replace the small workshop, production processes were changed enormously. The development of the steam engine led to the introduction of machine tools, mass-production, and specialisation within the work-force.

Piano making

Employees in piano making specialised in a range of activities: making soundboards, keyboards, hammers, actions, nameboards, etc. Commercial marketing developed alongside the popularisation of music and was concerned with making prices democratic by offering a wide variety of models. This range gradually reduced as models were standardised. The large piano making firms such as Érard, Pleyel, Henri Herz and Jean-Henri Pape opened real factories on the outskirts of Paris, and kept their old buildings in the centre of the city as venues for exhibitions and concerts. Famous pianists built up associations with the most important firms: Chopin chose Pleyel, whereas Liszt preferred Érard.

The frenetic pace of invention led to some interesting developments, such as the double escapement action, metal frames and the use of felt on the hammers, but a good many inventions had no future. National and international exhibitions were showcases for new inventions, and special models were built specifically for these industrial fairs. The builders were judged by an official jury, and received gold, silver and bronze medals, which they could mention next to the signature on their pianos.

124. Michel-Charles Fichot, *Piano making. Factory of Pleyel, Wolff and Co.*
Extract from *L'Illustration*, Paris, 1870

Mass production of violins

In the 19th century stringed instrument makers had to change radically many areas of their production due to the increasing imports of cheap violins. Up until this point it was mainly highly valuable violins that would have been found on the international market. Ordinary instruments were manufactured almost everywhere in Europe on a local basis. In the 19th century cheaper violins began to be mass produced in certain towns and villages where numerous stringed instrument makers had already been working in the 18th century. These locations were usually found near wooded mountainous areas, which could provide the necessary wood (pine or maple), and sufficient water power to drive the sawmills. The villages of Schönbach, Markneukirchen and Klingental lie to the west of the Armorican massif (the frontier between Saxony and Bohemia). Mittenwald lies on the frontier between Bavaria and the Tyrol, and Mirecourt is close to the Vosges.

These places already had a long-standing tradition of hand-crafted woodwork, and violin making became a part of this. Labour was also cheaper than in the towns. In Mittenwald there were mainly small family businesses, but large workshops were established in Markneukirchen and Klingental. As in other manufacturing industries, child labour was used until the beginning of the 20th century. It was rare that a worker, either in a large workshop or in the home, would work on, and complete, an entire instrument. Rather they were specialists in a specific area. A limited number of well-known families centralised the selling of the violins and their names can often be found on labels and stamps. Different family members would then set themselves up in the larger cities — for example, Jean-Baptiste and Nicolas-François Vuillaume, originally from Mirecourt, went respectively to Brussels and to Paris. Here, in addition to a limited number of special instruments, they would mainly sell far cheaper instruments, which had been made in their home village.

125. A luthier's workshop in Mirecourt, end of the 19th century. Post card.
Photo MIM, Brussels

Wind instrument manufacture

The division of activities in the manufacture of wind instruments gave rise to around twenty specialisations. There would be wood-turners, valve, key and mouthpiece makers, cabinetmakers, painters, polishers, assemblers and adjusters. The men were usually wood-turners and finishers and women were responsible for the polishing.

The extent to which a workshop was mechanised can be measured by the use they made of the steam engine. By 1847, Adolphe Sax had already equipped his Paris workshops with one such machine. By 1867, the firm Gautrot had twelve of them, both in its Paris workshop and at Château-Thierry. In 1871, Charles Mahillon installed a steam engine in Brussels. The aim of this extreme specialisation of labour and mechanised production was to achieve profitable production and competitive prices. This necessitated a concentration of production units and increased production within each of these units. For some builders production figures were very high. Adolphe Sax made some 40,000 instruments during his career.

However, small units continued to exist and produced hand-made instruments. One of these was Theobald Boehm in Munich. Boehm never had more than two collaborators. He was determined to continue making hand-crafted instruments, preferring quality to quantity. Between 1847 and 1858, he produced only 130 transverse flutes. His entire production numbered some 300.

126. Brass instrument factory of Victor-Charles Mahillon in Brussels. From *Zeitschrift für Instrumentenbau*, Leipzig, 1885

61. Experimental stringed instruments in the 19th and early 20th centuries

The new social and political context in Western Europe after 1800 had a profound effect on musical life. Concerts left the intimate aristocratic salons to take place in larger rooms where they had a new public, drawn from the bourgeoisie. This growth of public concerts led to the adaptation of instruments in order to make them more powerful. In parallel with this development there was much research with new forms and unusual materials. Experimental violins abandoned the classical form in the search for new structures: instruments with no angles, with bodies either flattened or convex lengthwise, or asymetrical or enlarged bodies. The number, form and place of the soundholes were modified and the strings passed over a fixed bridge. Some of these new ideas were borrowed from the guitar, which also underwent many modifications aimed at increasing the volume of the sound. Efforts were essentially concentrated on increasing the number of strings and enlarging the case, with reference to the antique lyre, the lute or the harp. All of these trials were rapidly abandoned and most have now almost been forgotten.

Most of the inventions made to improve the mechanism of the pedal harp suffered the same fate. However, in 1810 Sébastien Érard invented and patented the harp with a double shift pedal, considered as the most ingenious invention of the century in plucked stringed instrument making. Moreover, the present orchestral harp has not fundamentally changed since Érard.

The violino arpa

This experimental violin* was invented and built in 1873 by Thomas Zach on the instigation of the Hungarian Prince Gregor Stourdza. Several examples of this patented instrument have been conserved, but it met with no success. With strings of normal violin length, its body was oversized and of unusual shape in the hope of increasing the volume of its sound.

127. *Violino arpa*, **Thomas Zach, Vienna, 1873** (inv. M1359)

The dixtuor of Léon and Léo Sir

In order to enable the instruments of the string quartet to play in a more appropriate tessitura, the musician Léo Sir conceived and designed six additional instruments. His father, the violin maker Léon Sir, between 1908 and 1920 in Marmande (France), built instruments which he called sopranino, mezzo-soprano, contralto, tenor, baryton and double- or sub-bass. These considerably increased the range of colours available to the violin family, and the resulting string dixtuor played several concerts of works by Darius Milhaud and Arthur Honegger in Paris between the two world wars. The ensemble had an ephemeral success.

62. Innovations in 19th century wind instruments

In the course of the 19th century, woodwinds were given different systems of keys and many different kinds of valves were tried out on the instruments of the brass family. Theobald Boehm's* ring key system, introduced on the flute in 1832 and later to be used on the clarinet and on the saxophone was one of the most memorable inventions of the century.

The first valved brass instruments were made around 1818 by Friedrich Blühmel and Heinrich Stölzel. The cornet, a favourite instrument for amateur virtuosi, was the subject of many different valve experiments. In general, valves are of three types: simple tubular valves, the rotary valve and the double-cylinder valve.

The many experiments carried out on wind instruments were mainly influenced by industrial production: new techniques, materials, and concepts were used in the search for perfection. Boehm and Sax both found, in the parabolic form, a geometrical ideal which they reproduced in the head joint of the flute and of the saxophone respectively. Sax was particularly obsessed

by the parabola. He used it in a design of a concert hall in 1866 and, twenty years later, for making a bell. The revival of metal, especially brass, as an ideal material for musical instruments is typical of the 19th century. The saxophone, whose sound is produced by a thin reed, like certain woodwinds, was made in brass from the beginning. This is not as exceptional as it seems, for

128. Theobald Boehm, Munich, c. 1854.
© Münchner Stadtmuseum,
Grafiksammlung

129. Different types of pistons: B flat cornet, L. Bouvet, Paris, 1888; trumpet in F, A.G. Guichard, Paris, second quarter of the 19th century; trumpet, Charles-Joseph Sax, Brussels, mid-19th century (inv. M1302, M1309 & M1306)

clarinets, bassoons, and some double-reed instrument families like the sarrusophones and the rothphones were also made in brass.

The intense industrial development inspired many solutions to the problems of instrument building. The pistons in brass instruments, brought in around 1815-1818, were copied by Stölzel and Blühmel from a blast furnace mechanism that they saw in Silesia. Boehm, between 1839 and 1845, moved into the world of industrialised production. At this period, he was no longer making flutes and he became so enthralled by industrial metallurgy that he designed and built a blast furnace incinerator as well as a fire-box for locomotives.

63. Historical concerts

Until the middle of the 19th century, only contemporary music was played; the music of the past was a curiosity performed in 'historical concerts'. This taste for older music became stronger around the middle of the century. The revival of religious choral music started at the beginning of the 19th century. From the 1830s on, the harpsichord and viol were the instruments mostly used in historical concerts. Old keyboard instruments preoccupied personalities such as Carl Engel and Alfred J. Hipkins in the second half of the 19th century.

François-Joseph Fétis organised the first historical concerts in Paris in 1833, shortly before he became director of the Brussels Royal Music Conservatory.

After this, the series of concerts alternated between Paris and Brussels. The Brussels Musical Instruments Museum, founded in 1877, was also active. Victor-Charles Mahillon showed instruments from the collection at historical concerts organised at the Brussels Conservatory* between 1879 and 1890, but also in London in 1885, at the *Palais des Académies* in Brussels in 1886 and 1888 and at Bologna in 1888. In addition, Victor Mahillon made copies of old instruments for the concert of old Greek and Roman music given on 25 May 1896 at the Brussels Conservatory.

130. Miss Lunssens playing the 'antique' *kithara* on the occasion of a lecture given by Gevaert on 26 May 1886 at the Brussels Conservatory. Photo by the Géruzet brothers. MIM, Brussels

The programmes of these historical concerts included harpsichord pieces by Jean-Philippe Rameau, François Couperin, Johann Sebastian Bach, Mathias Van den Gheyn and Domenico Scarlatti, sonatas for the viol composed by Georg Friedrich Händel, J.S. Bach, Carl Philipp Emanuel Bach and Luigi Boccherini, arias by Jean-Baptiste Lully, Jean-Philippe Rameau and J.S. Bach, extracts from a flute concerto by Johann Joachim Quantz, a 'Sinfonia' from the opera *Euridice* by Jacopo Peri, and a mercenaries march arranged for a recorder ensemble.

From 1932, Safford Cape, who inherited his passion for old music from his father-in-law Charles Van den Borren, the Belgian musicologist, organised concerts of music from the Middle Ages for the Belgian radio.

In the 1960s, old music was increasingly successful. This could be seen in several ways: the growth in the number of old music groups, the interest in an 'authentic' interpretation, a deeper study of little-known repertoires, the foundation of instrument makers' workshops specialising in making copies of old instruments, the considerable expansion of the Renaissance and Baroque record market, the publication of books, etc.

64. Clavichords

The clavichord appeared in the early 15th century. This small but expressive instrument is usually built in either a rectangular or polygonal shape. The action is very simple: the strings are struck by small metal blades called tangents. This action allows the player to give much dynamic expression and also to use a sort of vibrato which the Germans called *Bebung*. In any case, because of the very small intensity of the sound, the clavichord was above all for intimate solo playing.

Two sorts of clavichords were built. In the older type, the fretted clavichord*, two, three or even four tangents struck the same strings at different points, thus producing sounds of different pitches. On this type of clavichord, it is

131. Workshop of Jan Van Hemessen, *Maria Magdalena at the clavichord*, Southern Low Countries, 1534. © Worcester Art Museum, Worcester, Massachussetts

This painting clearly shows the bent form of the key-levers, a characteristic of the fretted clavichord.

impossible to play two keys which use the same choir of strings. The unfretted clavichord, which appeared around the end of the 17th century, has a different pair of strings for each tangent.

The clavichord was played in Western Europe, especially in Germany, until the beginning of the 19th century. It was mostly considered as a practice instrument, especially for organists, and at first did not have its own specific literature. It was only in the second half of the 18th century that its expressive possibilities were recognised and that pieces were composed for this instrument. Carl Philipp Emanuel Bach, along with other composers, wrote many pieces for the clavichord.

The clavichord became obsolete at the beginning of the 19th century, but underwent a revival at the end of the 1880s, partly thanks to the musicologist, performer and maker Arnold Dolmetsch.

132. Polygonal clavichord, Italy, early 17th century (inv. M1620)

This fretted clavichord is the oldest of the collection of the MIM, and was probably made in Venice. Like many keyboard instruments of the period, it has a short octave.

65. Virginals, spinets and harpsichords

Virginals, spinets and harpsichords are plucked stringed instruments. They can be distinguished by the different forms of the case and the arrangement of the strings. The harpsichord* is wing-shaped with its strings in the same direction as the key-levers; the virginal* and spinet have a rectangular or polygonal case with the strings more or less parallel to the keyboard. The word 'virginal' was mostly used in the north of Europe and 'spinet' in the south. A clavicytherium is a vertical harpsichord on a stand.

The harpsichord was one of the favourite instruments during the Renaissance and Baroque periods. It was used as a solo instrument, as well as in the orchestra, the opera and in chamber music. Its repertoire is very large, from suites to toccatas, sonatas to concertos. Most composers, including Girolamo Frescobaldi, François Couperin, Jean-Philippe Rameau, Henry Purcell,

133. Paul-Joseph Delcloche, *Concert at the Castle of Seraing in the presence of Jean-Théodore of Baviere, Prince-Bishop of Liège, 1753.* © Bayerisches Nationalmuseum, Munich

From the 17th century the harpsichord was one of the favourite instruments for playing continuo (the accompanying of vocal or instrumental pieces from a figured bass).

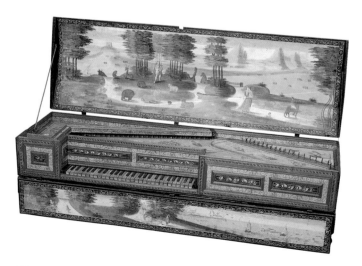

134. Rectangular virginal, Gabriel Townsend, London, 1641 (inv. M1591). Restored thanks to the sponsorship of Fortis AG

135. Hieronymus I Francken, *The Prodigal Son with the Courtisans*, Antwerp, c. 1580.
© Musée des Beaux-Arts, Nîmes

In the 16th and 17th centuries, the presence of musical instruments in paintings of the Low Countries almost always has a symbolic signification. Here, the keyboard instrument is an allegory of the union of a bourgeois family, but paradoxically it is also associated with libertine themes.

Georg Friedrich Händel or Johann Sebastian Bach wrote many pieces for this instrument. Domenico Scarlatti, for example, wrote 550 sonatas for this instrument.

A symbol of the aristocracy and the rich bourgeois, the harpsichord was a luxurious piece of furniture. It was an object of great care as much for its quality as for its often sumptuous decoration by famous painters or precious ornaments.

Despite their more limited musical resources, the spinet and the virginal were more well-known than the harpsichord because they were cheaper and smaller. Nevertheless, they were used mostly in private homes, more often by amateurs than professionals.

66. Harpsichord building traditions

In Europe, there were several important schools of harpsichord building, each with its own specific characteristics.

The Italian school

The Italian harpsichord, with its tapered and gracious form, was placed in an outer case which protected its light construction. It usually had one keyboard

136. Harpsichord, Giovanni Battista Boni, Cortona, 1619 (inv. M1603)

and one or two choirs of strings, each with its own register of jacks. The soundboard usually had a circular opening — the rose — with a delicately designed wood or parchment pattern. The lid and the exterior of the outer case were painted. A fine moulding crowned the sides of the instrument. Often, ivory buttons were placed on the side of the case or on the nameboard. The diatonic keys were usually covered in boxwood and the keyfronts decorated by parchment or boxwood. Most of the instruments have a short octave. In the 16th century, Venice was an important centre of harpsichord building.

The Flemish school

From the 17th century the role of Antwerp, a very important commercial and cultural crossroad, became predominant because of the renown of the prestigious Ruckers dynasty. The Flemish harpsichord can be distinguished from its Italian counterpart by its heavier form and more robust construction, which no longer needed an outer case to protect the instrument. The decoration is also very different: the outside of the case is often painted in imitation marble while the inside surfaces are ornamented with printed paper with patterns taken from Renaissance books. The interior of the lid is covered with paper imitating wood, enhanced by Latin sentences, either of a religious nature or relating to bourgeois morality. The soundboard is painted with flowers, leaves, fruit and birds: there is a lead rose representing an angel musician with the maker's initials on either side. The Flemish harpsichord has either one or two keyboards and two to four ranks of jacks.

Other European schools

Although the importance of the Flemish school was considerable in Europe, other European schools nevertheless have their own specific characteristics. The English specially liked the bentside or wing spinet, while in Germany, the Hamburg school made instruments with two or three keyboards and many stops.

137. Harpsichord combined with a virginal, Joannes Ruckers, Antwerp, 1619 (inv. M2935)

From the end of the 17th century, the lack of expressive possibilities of the harpsichord became a point of reproach. The 1773 letter to the *Journal de Musique* by the canon and organist of Nevers shows this clearly:

'Despite the inexhaustible resources which the harpsichord offers to the talented, one cannot but note that the equality of its sounds is a very real failing. This instrument, originally very simple, at first had only one keyboard, as in our spinets. For several centuries, it has more or less kept the same simplicity. After, someone imagined doubling the jacks on each key to give a little variation in the sound... Then the makers thought of putting in two keyboards, of which the upper played one rank of jacks and the lower both ranks. By this means, there was loud and soft, but the loud and the soft were always the same, with no way of graduating between the two. Later, a thousand inventions were made to amplify, to decorate, to improve the

138. Harpsichord, Hieronymus Albrecht Hass, Hamburg, 1734 (inv. M630)

instrument, but what should have been the aim, of graduating the sounds as nature and taste inspire a delicate ear and a sensitive soul, was never touched upon'.

Pushed to the background by the rise of the pianoforte, the harpsichord was to be forgotten from the beginning of the 19th century. Less than eighty years later, it came back on the scene and since then has become more and more well-known.

67. Demonstration actions

Stringed keyboard instruments can be divided into two groups: on one hand, plucked strings, with harpsichords, spinets and virginals; on the other, struck strings, with clavichords and pianos.

Clavichord action

Clavichord action is simple: each key has a small metal blade called the tangent. This tangent divides the string into two parts, of which the right hand part sounds between the bridge and the tangent, which momentarily becomes a bridge, thus determining the pitch. The left hand part is damped, as is the whole string on the release of the key.

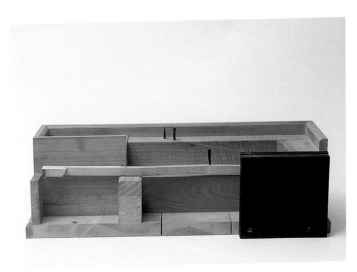

139. Clavichord action, Claude Kelecom, Brussels, MIM, 1990

Harpsichord, spinet and virginal action

When the key of a harpsichord, spinet or virginal is pressed, it tilts and pushes up a small piece of wood placed at its end, called a jack. This piece is equipped with a quill or leather plectrum that then plucks the string. Each key can activate one or several jacks which respectively pluck strings of different lengths, producing varying timbres called registers.

140. Harpsichord, spinet or virginal action, Claude Kelecom, Brussels, MIM, 1990

Piano action

Compared to that of the clavichord, piano action is extremely complex, with hundreds of patents. Nevertheless, all the different actions can be grouped in one or the other of the following categories: on the one hand, English or French actions, inspired by those of Bartolomeo Cristofori, the father of the piano, in which the hammer is attached to a fixed bar and 'pushed' towards the string; on the other, Austrian or German actions, in which the hammer,

141. Piano action, Bartolomeo Cristofori, Florence, 1709, reproduced by John Broadwood and Sons after plans by Scipione Maffei (inv. M1643)

articulated in a fork attached to the key, is 'pulled' towards the string. These two categories are easily distinguished: the heads of the hammers are directed towards the rear of the instrument in the English or French actions, and towards the front in the Austro-German actions.

The major inconvenience of the early actions — whether of English, French, German or Viennese origin — is due to the fact that in order to repeat a note the key has to be completely released and returned to its original position. This renders difficult any rapid repetition of a single note. In 1821 Sébastien Érard found the solution with the double escapement action which allowed the note to be repeated at any point in the key's descent.

This ingenious invention is still the basis of modern piano actions.

68. Psalteries and dulcimers

During the Middle Ages the instruments of Western Europe were greatly augmented by instruments from Persia and Arabia. These spread into Europe through Byzantium and Spain. Many varieties of plucked and struck psalteries reached us in this way and can now be seen in collections. The most common type has a series of strings fixed over a trapezoidal, flat-based sound box. Many of these small instruments are richly decorated in a style similar to that of the harpsichord, with painted or gilded tops. Others are embellished with precious woods.

142. Cimbalom, O. Weidlich, Budapest, second half of the 19th century (inv. M2036)

143. Dulcimer, Aegidius Huysmans, Antwerp, middle of the 17th century (inv. M2945)

Psalteries and dulcimers were to be found at all social levels. In medieval times the strings formed a diatonic scale, each producing only one note. In the 18th century these instruments were totally chromatic and a bridge divided the strings into two vibrating sections, often at an interval of a fifth. In order to augment the sound volume, more strings were added for each note. In the 19th century the range was increased still further. The dulcimer with an extended range became very popular in Hungary. It was developed still further and became a true concert instrument — the cimbalom*. The simplest versions remained in use as popular instruments throughout Europe.

Aegidius Huysmans and the dulcimer in the Southern Low Countries

The dulcimer attributed to Aegidius Huysmans* is, for its period, a highly developed instrument with a chromatic range. Presumably it was much enjoyed by the Antwerp bourgeoisie. The harpsichord maker Joannes Couchet also made dulcimers.

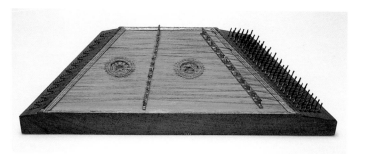

144. Psaltery, Joseph Alsina, Barcinona, Canary Islands, 1779 (inv. M1486)

Pablo Minguet and the Spanish psaltery with extended range

In Madrid in 1754, Minguet set down a set of rules for the playing of the dulcimer with finger plectra or *dediles*. This was the most common playing technique in the Spanish Empire. An 1779 instrument by Joseph Alsina of Barcinona* bears a great resemblance in size and in shape to the work of Minguet as seen in engravings.

69. Guitars

The oldest examples of guitars in more or less original condition date only from the 17th century. They are of inestimable value for our knowledge of the structure and development of the instrument. At that time the guitar had five pairs of strings and accompanied singers of all social classes. With the

145. Two five-course guitars of Giorgio Jungmann, Genoa, 1633, and of Matteo Sellas, Venice, first half of the 17th century (inv. M3183 & M550)

146. Lyre guitar, François Roudhloff-Mauchand, Paris, first quarter of the 19th century (inv. M266)

increasing popularity of public concerts at the beginning of the 19th century, several changes were made — the sound box was enlarged and a sixth string was added. Experiments were also made with the tuning of the instrument. The *chitarra battente*, with double or triple metal strings, is the folk version of the guitar. Accompanying chords are strummed with a plectrum. This instrument was found mainly in Italy in the 18th and 19th centuries.

Matteo Sellas in Venice

Matteo Sellas was the most famous descendant of an instrument making family from Allgäu in the north of Italy in the 17th century. From the middle of the 16th century many lute makers crossed the Alps, fleeing from the war. Some twenty or so Sellas instruments have survived, thanks largely to the skilful level of decoration that they show*. The rose of the harpsichord maker Jean-Henry Hemsch is a later addition.

Manufacture and use of the guitar in the Southern Low Countries

Financial records of many towns show that payments were regularly made during the 15th and 16th centuries to guitarists who played for processions. Documents printed in Antwerp also mention the instrument. In 1648 Francesco Corbetta dedicated his *Varii Scherzi di sonate per la chitarra spagnola* to the Archduke and Archduchess Albert and Isabella and thus contributed to the spreading popularity of the instrument amongst the local aristocracy. We still have several 18th century guitars that came from this region.

The fashion of the lyre guitar in France

In the last quarter of the 18th century and the beginning of the 19th century a fleeting passion for all things from Antiquity led to a fashion amongst the bourgeoisie and the aristocracy for guitars in the shape of an antique lyre*. The lyre guitar had six single strings and was thus a precursor of the 19th century romantic guitar.

70. Citterns

The cittern is a plucked instrument which achieved great popularity in the 16th and 17th centuries. It existed in several sizes and was often shown in allegorical and popular scenes. It differs from the lute and other Renaissance plucked instruments by its having metal strings and being played with a plectrum.

From 1650, its popularity declined, except in England where it continued to play an important and lasting role in chamber music. During the second half of the 18th century, a modified version of the instrument met with particular success in Northern France and in England. It had a deeper sound box and was to replace the lute, which fell into disuse.

The archcittern, with an additional range of bass strings, sometimes replaced the theorbo, the bass instrument of the lute family, also fallen into disuse.

147. Detail of a cittern, Gérard-J. Deleplanque, Lille, 1775 (inv. M537)

148. Cittern player. Detail of Arthur Davis, *The Maynard Family in the Park at Walton*, Essex. 1759-1761. National Gallery of Art, The Mellon Collection, Washington DC; © Board of Trustees, National Gallery of Art, 1998

Gérard-J. Deleplanque (active between 1755 and 1790)

Today we still have several dozen citterns made by Deleplanque in his Lille workshop. The choice of wood is very classical, but some of the instruments are delicately decorated and have beautiful roses*. Deleplanque also made guitars, pandoras, and a number of bowed stringed instruments.

The English guitar

The modified cittern was so appreciated in England that it became known as the *English guitar*. It was successfully introduced into bourgeois circles and was played above all by ladies*. An ingenious tuning mechanism was added very soon, allowing the strings to be tuned by means of small, spiral keys. In London in 1784, Christian Claus patented a mechanism in which a keyboard activated small hammers that struck the strings*. The English cittern gave rise to the Portuguese *guitarra*.

149. English guitar with keyboard, Longman & Broderip, London, second half of the 18th century (inv. M1552)

71. Mandolins

The Neapolitan mandolin* is the most well-known version of this small, popular instrument which was a source of inspiration for many composers from the mid-18th century. It was preferred above all for romantic serenades, but was also used to accompany arias in serious operas. The type of music written for the mandolin stemmed from the tuning of the instrument, in fifths, like the violin. This partly explains the reason for its increasing popularity at the end of the 18th century. The Neapolitan tradition of melodious tunes and the flourishing culture of the time were both major factors as well in the rising popularity of this plucked stringed instrument. In the 18th century the mandolin was still essentially a hand-crafted instrument with fine decoration. Mass production came about towards 1900 due to the rise in interest being shown around Europe in the mandolin as a popular instrument. A small model of the mandolin was played in the streets but alongside of this a whole family of mandolins were used in orchestras or *estudiantinas*.

The Milanese variety is older and bears a far greater resemblance to the lute. It has five or six pairs of gut strings, plucked with the fingers. Vivaldi wrote

150. Neapolitan mandolin, Giovanni Vinaccia, Naples, 1767 (inv. M530)

151. Mandola, Luigi Embergher, Rome, 1925 (inv. 91.066)

his *Concerto per mandolino* for the girls' school of the *Ospedale della Pietà* in Venice for this instrument. There is little information available on the larger 18th century mandola. The sound box is similar to that of the lute, and it has a long slender neck. In the 20th century the mandola* was used for the bass part in mandolin ensembles.

The colascione

The *colascione* was developed in the south of Italy and shows the influence of some elements of the long-necked Arab lute. It has a very small sound box, a long neck and two or three strings that are played with a plectrum. Around 1750, a

152. *Mezzo-colascione*, Gosewijn Spyker, Amsterdam, 1759 (inv. M1568)

smaller version became popular, its popularity spreading throughout Western Europe. The *mezzo-colascione** attributed to Gosewijn Spyker is such an instrument.

The Vinaccia family

The evolution of the Neapolitan mandolin to its present form, with the deep sound box and a soundboard angled under the bridge, is largely attributed to a member of the Vinaccia family. The Vinaccia dynasty was prominent from the beginning of the 18th century up to the end of the 19th century. The earliest instruments have a refined shape and the work is of the highest quality, both in terms of the choice of materials and of the finishing details.

72. Florentine intermedii

During the Renaissance, Italian courts organised lavish entertainments, partly to show off their social status and also to demonstrate their wide cultural interests. The Medici family used it as part of their political activity. Music, dance and theatre were all closely interlinked. In theatrical productions musical interludes or intermedii were interspersed between the acts as light entertainment. The content of these intermedii was influenced by the current humanist theories on music and art, in which mythology played a large part.

153. Scenery for the fourth Intermedio of *La Pellegrina*, engraving by B. Buontalenti.
Extract from H.M. Brown, *Sixteenth Century Instrumentation: The Music for the Florentine Intermedii*, 1973

154. Rose of a *chitarrone*, Matheus Buchenberg, Rome, 1610 (inv. M1570)

155. Tenor trombone, Hanns Hainlein, Nuremberg, 1668 (inv. M1265)

As the 16th century progressed, the thematic unity of the whole spectacle became more and more important. A great deal of attention was paid to the staging of the plays, and spectacular special effects were incorporated thanks to the use of complicated machinery.

The Florentine intermedii of 1589

The best known intermedii, and those for which we still have the music with indications for instrumentation, were those written on the occasion of the wedding of Ferdinand de Medici and Christine de Lorraine, the granddaughter of Henry III, King of France, and of Catherine de Medici. This was a political marriage and the *La Pellegrina** interludes constituted the high point of three weeks of festivities. 286 costumes were made, based on classical models. The music for the comedy was the work of young, talented composers such as Cavalieri, Caccini, Marenzio and Peri. The prologue sings the praises of the harmony between the bride and the groom. The first intermezzo portrays the harmony of the spheres, as described by Plato, and the six others take their themes from Greek mythology and sing of the power of music.

The musical instruments in La Pellegrina

Nearly all of the choruses and madrigal solos have instrumental accompaniments. The instrumentation is very varied. Stringed instruments play a dominant role with instruments of the lute and viola da gamba families appearing in all registers. The *lira da braccio* accompanied the high voices, while the harp reinforced the continuo parts. The repeated use of the violin was a new element. Cornetts regularly took the soprano part and trombones* were used to add dramatic atmosphere to certain scenes. The harpsichord and spinet are conspicuous by their absence in this spectacle. On the other hand, a small positive organ doubles the solo vocal parts and a regal organ, with its nasal tones (see also no. 76), was used in the ensemble pieces.

73. Early violin making techniques

Beginning in the 19th century, violin making methods became more and more uniform, so that today's modern system is the only one still in use. Previously, the different processes could be grouped into two principal techniques. The first was based on fitting one part of the instrument into another. It was mainly used by itinerant musicians*. It is this technique, probably the older, that determined the shape of the violin. The neck is not glued to the body but fitted into it: the ribs slide into grooves cut into the back and neck; at each of the four corners the ends of the ribs are glued directly together and not on to blocks of wood. It is surely this technique that gave the violin even today its rounded shoulders (the ribs are placed in a perpendicular groove in the neck), sharp corners (ribs glued together at the ends), and table and back overlapping the sides by several millimetres (fitting into the slot in the perimeter of the back). This technique prevailed until the 18th century in much of Europe, gradually disappearing between 1750 and 1830.

The second method of construction was inspired by that of the lute, and most likely begun by the lute makers themselves. 'Lute maker' (*luthier* and *liutaio*) is still the word in French and Italian for a violin maker. In this method glued joints form the major part of the assemblage. As with the lute, the violin is fashioned on a form. The neck and end-pin blocks are placed, then the four corner blocks to which are glued the segments of the sides (ribs). The neck is not fitted into the body but glued and then nailed to the upper block. Thin wooden linings increase the gluing surface between the ribs and the back and table. Long joints

156. Bass violin, Hans Krouchdaler, Oberbalm, Switzerland, 1654 (inv. M1442)

17th century violin making in this region was among the most archaic in Europe.

and extended or fragile surfaces may be reinforced with parchment or paper. This making method, used among others by the famous makers in Cremona, became synonymous with quality from the end of the 17th century. It replaced the traditional technique in many areas and forms the basis of modern violin making.

74. Bows

For today's player, the bow is as important as the instrument itself. Precise balancing of the different parameters of length, weight, shape, flexibility, and height of the head and the frog (the grip) can considerably increase technical possibilities in playing. Today's bow is perfectly adapted to the virtuoso violin repertoire after 1800.

Over the centuries bowmaking techniques evolved parallel to those of the stringed instruments themselves. Illustrations of 16th century violins show a short, convex bow, with the hair tightened by pressure from the player's thumb. This was suitable for the dance music of the period. In the 17th and 18th centuries we find bows with hair that can be more or less tightened with a notched piece or a mobile handle. The convex shape is thus progressively diminished and the head slightly raised. This bow is especially efficient for quick, repeated notes and the florid ornaments of baroque music. Along with the evolution of the shape, special attention began to be given in the 17th and 18th centuries to the materials used. Fine quality bows are made of high-density wood like amourette. To make it lighter, the stick is often fluted over most of its length.

Around 1770, several innovations, traditionally attributed to the French bowmaker Tourte the father, made a real break with the past. First, the hair was tightened by a screw moving the frog along a groove: second, the head was raised much higher. François Tourte continued to perfect his father's ideas, arriving at the modern bow used today. To him is also attributed the use of pernambuco, a Brazilian wood preferred by modern bowmakers.

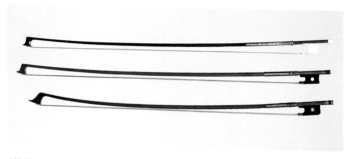

157. Bows for violin, viola and violoncello: Nicolas Léonard Tourte, Paris, c. 1770-1780; Dominique Peccatte, Paris, 1850-1860; Alfred Joseph Lamy?, Paris, for H. Darche, 1890-1925 (inv. M507, 3478 & 3496)

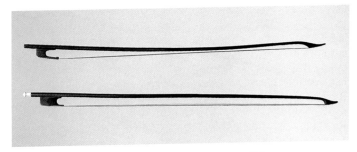

158. Baroque bows for treble and bass viols (inv. JT078 and M511)

The Tourte family

Recent research has cast some doubts on the inventions of Tourte the father. Nicolas Pierre Tourte is known with certitude only to have been a *luthier*. His sons Nicolas Léonard and François Xavier were probably the pioneers of the transition from the baroque to the raised-head bow design. The example of Nicolas Léonard Tourte, signed 'L. Tourte' is a transitional model*.

The Ernest Tschaggeny collection

During his life, this enlightened amateur assembled a fabulous collection of bows from the 19th and early 20th centuries. After his death in 1920, his brother Frédéric donated the collection to the MIM. As well as a few English bows, it includes a great quantity of French bows. Specimens by Fonclause, Maire, Lupot, Pajot, Peccatte, Simon, Voirin and others show sustained and exceptional quality during almost a century*.

75. The violin maker's workshop

This space recreates the workshop of a traditional violin maker. The furniture is rudimentary: a work-bench, stools and shelves for tools. A small stock of wood is necessary for building and repairing. Hung on the wall are moulds and forms for shaping and fashioning instruments. Note familiar tools such as saws, knives, chisels, planes, compass and different sized clamps. In addition, the violin maker uses special tools like an iron to bend the ribs, a gauge to measure the thickness of the soundboard and back, and an engraving tool for the purfling. A shaper and borer for the pegs and their holes and a pointed tool for placing the sound-post finish the job of making the instrument playable. Alcohol, oil, glue, varnish, rosin and pigments complete the equipment. After the varnish is prepared, it is applied in another room which is isolated from dust.

From the 19th century onwards Belgian violin makers conformed to traditional French making practices. At this period French makers set up shop in Belgium. This was the case of Nicolas-François Vuillaume (Jean-Baptiste's brother) and Charles-Claude-François Darche. They were essentially inspired by Italian models. Many unfinished instruments were sent from their home base at Mirecourt and finished and adjusted in the makers' own workshops in Belgium. In these small workshops they made new instruments as well as repairs. The best known makers in Liège were the Bernards and Emile Heynberg, while the Darche family dominated Brussels, especially from the end of the 19th century.

The Bernards: a Liège family of violin makers

After a four-year apprenticeship at the house of Gand and Bernardel in Paris, the young André Bernard (1869-1959) founded his own workshop in his native Liège in 1893, under the sign 'À la Guitare Royale'. Two of his sons succeeded him: Joseph Bernard (1911-1940) and Jacques Bernard (1919-1992), to whom the MIM owes its exhibit of the family workshop*.

159. View of the Bernard workshop reconstituted at the MIM

The construction of a modern violin

Since the 19th century, violins are built in basically the same way all over the world. Modern technique is a variant of classical Italian practice, which stems from lute making. The quartersawn soundboard and back, respectively of pine and maple, are fashioned with gouges and finished with small planes and scrapers. On their perimeter is inlaid purfling, thin threads of black wood sandwiched around a thread of natural wood. The neck and sides (ribs) are of maple. The ribs are first curved with heat and water, then glued and held in place around wooden blocks. The neck goes onto the upper block. Under the soundboard, beneath the lowest string, is glued the bassbar. Another important piece takes its place under the highest string. This is the sound-post, a thin dowel inserted through the F-holes between the soundboard and back, placed under one of the feet of the bridge. It not only makes for greater solidity, but also helps transmit vibrations from the soundboard to the rest of the box. To finish, the instrument is given several coats of varnish to protect the wood from dust and perspiration.

76. Organs

The organ is one of the best-known keyboard instruments of Western Europe, as well as being the oldest. The large organs played in churches and concert halls are famous, while smaller instruments, specially conceived for palaces and bourgeois salons, remain less well-known.

The oldest type of European organ is probably the portative*. This is a small instrument, easily carried, and essentially conceived for monodic music. The development of polyphonic music led to the virtually systematic exclusion of the portative organ. A few literary sources bear witness to the existence of this instrument up to the beginning of the 20th century.

Other small organs (positives) played an important part, especially as instruments for accompanying polyphonic music. The positive organ kept its place during the 18th and 19th centuries, mostly for domestic use. It was mostly found in Protestant countries as an instrument for accompanying domestic psalm singing or for use in small churches.

A salon organ is usually placed in a piece of furniture in the form of a writing desk or cabinet. The evolution of the salon organ was completely different from that of the church organ or, from the 19th century, the large concert-hall organ. Despite its limited possibilities, the salon organ presents different timbres. Frequently half-stops are used. These half-stops divide a rank of pipes so that they can be played in either the treble or the bass; the treble and the bass pipes can be of different types. During the second half of the 19th century, the small organ gradually gave way to the harmonium, an instrument more easily bought by both amateurs and churches.

The regal

The regal* is a less well-known type of organ. It usually has just one rank of reed pipes. It was used in operas for special sound effects, as well as for accompanying services and choir practices, mostly in German Reformed churches.

The claviorganum and vielle organisée (Italian lira organizzata)

Sometimes the organ is found combined with another instrument; most often a positive organ with a harpsichord, known as a claviorganum. The *vielle*

160. Portative organ *nimfali*, France, late 19th century. Former attribution: Italy, 17th century (inv. M455)

This unique instrument is a reconstruction of a portative organ made at the end of the 19th century by the famous organologist Auguste Tolbecque, who worked from written and iconographic sources to reassemble different historic elements.

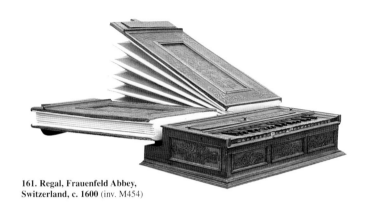

**161. Regal, Frauenfeld Abbey,
Switzerland, c. 1600** (inv. M454)

162. *Vielle organisée*, **César Pons, Grenoble, c. 1770** (inv. M552)

*organisée**, or a combination of the hurdy-gurdy and a positive organ is much
more rare. This type of instrument appeared around 1735 and was relatively
successful in France in the second half of the 18th century.

77. Harps

In Western Europe the harp developed from the small instrument of the troubadours to become the large orchestral instrument, while keeping its role as an accompanying instrument. In the 16th century the musical potential of the portable instrument, on which each string could only produce a single note, began to seem insufficient in the light of the increasing importance of instrumental music. The delicate tuning necessary on certain strings to enable the instrument to play in a variety of keys was made easier by the addition of hooks on the neck*. Around 1720 this system was mechanised and led to the development of the single action pedal harp*.

The harp enjoyed a huge success in the second half of the 18th century, particularly in France, where it became the darling of the aristocracy. The encyclopedias were full of the minutest details. However, it was only with the ingenious improvements made by Sébastien Érard that the harp became an instrument capable of playing in all keys. In 1810 Érard invented a device which meant that each string could be raised two semitones by using pedals.

163. Detail of a harp with hooks, Georg Offman? Germany, 1739 (inv. M1497)

164. Pedal harp, Cousineau father and Son, Paris, c. 1800 (inv. M246)

165. Chromatic harp, Pleyel, Wolff, Lyon and Co, Paris, end of the 19th century. Donation by the Friends of the MIM (inv. 2000.01)

Harp decorated in the art nouveau style, with an integrated tuning system, from the early range of Pleyel harps.

The chromatic harp around 1900

Around 1895, Gustave Lyon of the Paris firm Pleyel, invented the orchestral chromatic harp*. The instrument had a range of six and a half octaves with two rows of crossed strings. The idea of using one string for each semitone had already been used, with varying success, around 1600, as in the Italian invention called the *arpa doppia*. Lyon's chromatic harp had a separate string for each semitone, making all modulations possible, as on the piano. It was immediately a huge success and its history is closely linked to Belgian musical life. In 1900, Gevaert, then the director of the Brussels Royal Music Conservatory, was the first to create a course for the chromatic harp (which still exists today). In Paris this course appeared only three years later. Great composers such as Claude Debussy wrote for the chromatic harp. It was, however, the pedal harp of Érard which finally became the favoured instrument and by 1930 production of the chromatic harp had ceased.

78. The hall of mirrors

This room brings together some instruments which are especially beautiful, curious or extraordinary.

Bible regal

This is a small and very rare reed organ. It is conceived in such a way that when the instrument is folded up it resembles a large book. In the interior are two bellows, a series of pipes and the keyboard. The sound is produced by metal reeds, amplified by short conical resonators.

166. Bible regal, anonymous, South Germany?, c. 1700 (inv. M2703)

Ruckers-Taskin harpsichord

This harpsichord, attributed for a long time to Hans Ruckers on the basis of its signed rose, is probably a French instrument from the end of the 17th century. The paintings which ornament the lid and the case show a series of towns conquered by Louis XIV between 1667 and 1681. Drawings and a painting by Adam Frans van der Meulen have clearly served as models for the painters of his workshop to realise this decoration. In 1774 the harpsichord received a *ravalement* (enlargement) from the hand of Pascal Taskin. It was probably Taskin who incorporated Flemish elements into the soundboard. In 1904 the instrument was revised in Paris by Louis Tomasini who, amongst other interventions, provided it with its present stand.

167. Ruckers-Taskin harpsichord, France?, end of 17th century (inv. 3848). Paintings restored thanks to the Roi Baudouin Foundation

Clavicytherium by Albert Delin

Active in Tournai during the second half of the 18th century, Albert Delin is represented in the MIM by three instruments, one of which is this very fine clavicytherium, or vertical harpsichord, constructed in the tradition of the Antwerp school. The decoration of his instruments is sober but refined. The idea of a vertical harpsichord dates from as early as the 15th century, but it is rarely treated as simply and ingeniously as in this version by Delin. The tone quality of his instrument is exceptional, enhanced by the vertical position of the soundboard.

168. Clavicytherium, Albert Delin, Tournai, 1751 (inv. M554)

Pyramid piano by Christian Ernst Friderici

This is one of the earliest upright pianos ever built. Its structure is derived from that of the clavicytherium. The case of inlaid wood from different sources echoes the aesthetic of the Louis XV style. A key individual in the beginning of piano making, Friderici was long considered the inventor of the square and the upright piano. A maker of organs and keyboard instruments, he was already famous during his lifetime with composers and musicians as well as with theoreticians. The principal keyboard instrument in the home of Mozart's parents during the composer's childhood and adolescence was a Friderici harpsichord. The house also contained a Friderici clavichord. It is known that C.P.E. Bach owned a clavichord and a square piano made by Friderici.

169. Pyramid piano, Christian Ernst Friderici, Gera, Saxony, 1745 (inv. M1631)

Grand piano by Érard Frères

This magnificent pianoforte 'in the form of a new model of the harpsichord', conserved in its original state, dates from 1820. It was made by Sébastien Érard, a French maker considered to be one of the most talented and important in the history of the piano. It is to him that we owe, among other things, the invention of the double escapement action, the basis of modern piano action, which makes possible the rapid repetition of notes. The instrument presented here is one of the rare surviving examples that uses the stirrup action, a technique invented just before that of the double escapement.

170. Grand piano, Érard Frères, Paris, 1820
(inv. 98.011). Restored thanks to the sponsorship of Fortis AG

Lyre piano

The lyre piano derives its name from its case in the form of a giant lyre. It is, in fact, a grand piano placed vertically on a stand. This quite peculiar model of vertical piano, which seems specific to Berlin, was apparently invented by a builder named Sylig, active in Berlin during the first years of the 19th century. It was built in limited numbers until around 1850, thus rivalling other vertical grand piano models like the giraffe or pyramid pianos. The instrument presented here is unsigned but could be the work of J.B. Schleip, a pupil of Sylig.

171. Lyre piano, anonymous, Berlin, c. 1825
(inv. 99.001). Acquired thanks to the sponsorship of the Etex Group

Claviharp by Christian Dietz

Although the claviharp's form resembles that of the giraffe piano, it is a keyboard instrument whose strings are plucked, not struck, by small leather-covered hooks, activated by the keyboard. It is often equipped with one or several pedals that allow modifications of timbre. The claviharp was invented and patented in Paris in 1814 by the German engineer Johann Christian Dietz, a prolific inventor of musical instruments, amongst other things. The claviharp exposed here is the work of his grandson Christian, a Brussels resident. Played in concerts at the end of the 19th century, this instrument enjoyed a certain success. It was claimed that even a highly attentive listener could not distinguish it from a normal harp.

172. Claviharp, Christian Dietz, Brussels, end of 19th century (inv. 3343)

Two bass viols

The two bass viols in this hall are first and foremost instruments sumptuously decorated. Today, the instrument attributed to Caspar Tieffenbrucker is no longer considered as being from the 16th century. It keeps, however, its historical importance. This viol was apparently assembled for a collector, at the beginning of the 19th century, from pieces of old instruments. The marvellous decoration*, representing a map of Paris in marquetry on the back of the instrument, led to the belief that the instrument had belonged to the French King François I. This viol is mentioned for the first time in 1827; since then, it has continually been cited and reproduced as one of the most remarkable 'old' stringed instruments.

173. Detail of the bass viol called 'the map of Paris' (marquetry), Paris, 19th century (inv. M1427)

The bass viol by Joachim Tielke* is not only a collector's object, but is also playable. Tielke (1641-1719) is considered to be the most famous viol maker of his time. His instruments, often magnificently decorated, are renowned for the quality of their sound.

174. Bass viol, Joachim Tielke, Hamburg, 1701 (inv. M229)

Luxurious violin

This violin has many characteristics of the Baroque period: the short neck is aligned with the body and has a small fingerboard. Unusual materials have been used: the bottom is made of a particular type of ebony; the sides and the fingerboard are in tortoiseshell; the scroll, pegbox and tuning pegs are in ivory. It is not certain that this violin is really from the 18th century. It is possibly a decorative instrument made in the old style.

Column recorder by Hans Rauch

There is a certain mystery about the column recorder. There are only five extant examples in the world, all made by the South German Hans Rauch, who was active around the middle of the 16th century. Was the instrument conceived for an amateur with a passion for Antiquity? The mouthpiece is behind the column.

Bass clarinet by Nicola Papalini

Papalini's bass clarinet elegantly answers the needs of the clarinettist who wishes the bass register quickly to be available. Papalini called himself an *inventore*, but he is rather a designer, in the modern sense of the term, when one takes into consideration the functional and ergonomic form that he thought up for his bass clarinet. Only six of these instruments now exist.

175. Bass clarinet, Nicola Papalini, Chiaravalle, Italy, beginning of 19th century (inv. M940)

Crystal transverse flute by Claude Laurent

Claude Laurent, active in Paris between 1805 and 1848, succeeded in making transverse flutes in crystal. They were appreciated for their great resistance to temperature changes. His patent is dated 1806.

Trombone with seven bells by Adolphe Sax

The trombone with seven bells seems to be a play with forms. In fact, it is simply the logical conclusion of putting into practice the principle of one air column for each fundamental note. With Sax's invention, the sliding tube was no longer necessary, as each valve corresponded to a position of the sliding valve. Sax patented his invention of the seven-belled trombone in 1852, then improved this design in 1859.

176. Trombone with seven bells, Adolphe Sax, Paris, c. 1890 (inv. M1288)

Serpent chandelier

This chandelier made of serpents comes from the brass band of the Belgian town of Puurs, where it was indeed used as a chandelier before the MIM purchased it. The serpents date from the end of the 18th and the beginning of the 19th century. Before their new life as a chandelier, they were used as bass instruments in bands or to accompany church music. The sun and the crescent formed part of the Turkish crescent around which this chandelier was made.

177. Serpent chandelier, Puurs, Antwerp, end of 18th century - beginning of 19th century (inv. M2017)

Yaka slit drums

These small anthropomorphic slit drums are not used as instruments for signalling, but rather as fetishes and for divination. The Yaka of the Congo call them *mukoku*.

'The carved head of the *mukoku* personifies the soothsayer and serves as a link towards their ancestors for their role as mediators for sickness, illness and death. The closed eyes may allude to interior vision and to the soothsayer's dreams which see beyond the appearances of everyday life into the world of desire, black magic and sorcery' (A.P. Bourgeois).

178. Slit drums from Yaka, Congo (inv. LS 21, 75.040, 77.028/29/30 & 70.026)

79. Early pianos

From the end of the 17th century more and more interest was shown in finding ways in which the harpsichord could be made more expressive and have a greater range of tone. In actual fact the harpsichord player could not alter the volume of his instrument, no matter how hard he attacked the keys. Harpsichord makers came up with different systems to get round this disadvantage — they added a second keyboard and new registers. However, it was Bartolomeo Cristofori, harpsichord maker to Prince Ferdinand of Medici, who found the solution. In 1698, he invented a harpsichord on which the strings were no longer plucked by plectra, but were struck by hammers. He thus created the first *pianoforte* — on which a whole range of dynamic variations from *pianissimo* to *fortissimo* were possible. Cristofori's new instrument was described in an Italian periodical translated and published in Germany, and gradually the instrument spread throughout the whole of Europe.

179. Grand piano, Johann Andreas Stein, Augsburg, 1786
(inv. M1634). Restored thanks to the sponsorship of Fortis AG

This piano is similar to those used by Mozart in the 1780s, of which he sings the praises in a letter addressed to his father in 1777.

180. Edouard Renard, *La salle de concert de la firme Pleyel, Wolff et Cie à Paris*.
From *L'Illustration*, Paris, 1855

In 1830, the piano making firm Pleyel inaugurated their first public concert hall with the aim of promoting artists, and also their own pianos. It was here in 1832, that Chopin, little known at the time by the Parisian public, gave his first concert and here too that he was heard for the last time, a few months before his death on 16 February 1848.

181. Grand piano, Sébastien Érard, Paris, 1805 (inv. 74.003)

Many musicians had an Érard piano. The order books of the company show that the piano no. 28, made in 1800, was intended for Haydn, and no. 133, made in 1803, was for Beethoven. It was on this piano that Beethoven composed several important works including the Waldstein and Appassionata sonatas.

National schools of piano making

Each school of instrument making was quick to develop its own specialties, whether it was in the field of cabinetmaking or in improvements to the action. They each had their own followers and critics. Pianos of the Vienna school, such as those of Johann Andreas Stein*, with their light touch and clear sound, won praise from many musicians and composers, including Mozart. The English pianos, on the other hand, won favour for their more robust mechanism and powerful sound. Beethoven was known to be attached to the Broadwood piano given to him by the London firm in 1817. In France, Chopin was to choose a Pleyel piano*. Although Liszt may initially have preferred the Érard piano* with its renowned double escapement action, which greatly improved key repetition, he was later to turn to more powerful instruments such as those of Bösendorfer*, Bechstein and Steinway, pianos which could withstand his powerful attack.

182. Grand piano, Ignaz Bösendorfer, Vienna, c. 1845 (inv. 75.010)

80. Different types of piano

From the early 1720s some piano makers began to place the piano action in a rectangular case, similar to that of the clavichord. This instrument was called the square piano*. Although these are no longer made, they were very popular from the end of the 18th century to around 1840, and their production was ten times greater than that of grand pianos or upright pianos. Intended mainly for piano lovers and the bourgeoisie, the square piano was nonetheless much appreciated by composers and the aristocracy.

The manufacture of upright pianos, in the present sense of the word, did not begin until 1810, although the idea of a vertical piano goes back to the beginning of the 18th century. The aim of the manufacturers was to produce a piano which would take up less space than the grand piano, but which had the same quality of sound. Manufacturers came up with a whole host of original, and some totally fanciful, ideas, which showed real inventiveness — the cabinet piano*, the pyramid piano, the giraffe piano, the lyre piano, the dog kennel piano, or the console piano. From 1850 onwards the industrialisation of certain manufacturers led to an increased standardisation of models. Only the upright piano* and the grand piano* have survived to our days.

183. Square piano, Clermont, Berden and Co, Brussels, c. 1840 (inv. 81.006)

From the 1840s the production of square pianos dropped dramatically. The square piano had, over the years, become larger and larger and, in the end, was almost as cumbersome as the grand piano, without the benefit of the same quality of sound. It had lost its main advantage — its compact form — and towards 1860 it was replaced definitively by the upright piano. Interestingly, the latter has taken the opposite road and has become smaller.

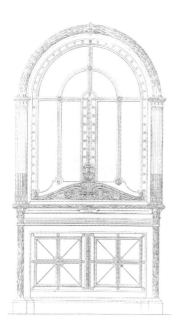

184. T.J. Suys, *Cabinet piano, Jean Groetaers and Sons*, **Brussels, 1830. Engraving.**
© KBR, Brussels, S1 23157/8

This instrument was apparently shown at the National Exhibition of industrial products in 1830 and 1835. In the 19th century exhibitions provided ideal showcases for the manufacturers to exhibit their newest inventions. The instruments were exceptionally well decorated. This cabinet piano was built by the firm Groetaers and Sons after a design by Suys, court architect of the time.

185. The music rooms of institutions for young ladies in Belgium, c. 1900. Post card.
Collection Jean Ferrard

During the 19th century the piano became a necessary bourgeois status symbol — a mark of social distinction. Piano study was an indispensable part of the education of any young lady of good family.

186. Grand piano, Pleyel, Lyon and Co. Drawn by Paul Follot, Paris 1925
(inv. 99.008)

81. Harmoniums

At the end of the 18th century, attempts to vary the sound of the organ (by definition, fixed) were based on a series of experiments on free reed keyboard instruments. At the beginning of the 19th century several makers, including Johann Nepomuk Maelzel, Anton Haeckl and Gabriel-Joseph Grenié, with his expressive organ (1810), started to become seriously interested by this problem. Around 1845 in Paris Théodore-Achille Müller made an expressive organ in which free reeds were associated with resonators. Following the example of his colleagues, Aristide Cavaillé-Coll made his own research, but rather in the path of the harmonium. In his *poïkilorgue**, the left pedal controls the quantity of wind, while the right pedal controls the wind pressure.

The use of free reeds can be applied, on the one hand, to keyboard instruments like the harmonium and its variations (*physharmonica*, *poïkilorgue*, *serafine* or *harmoniphon*) or on the other hand to experimental instruments, especially the melophone and the cecilium. Later free reeds were also used in mechanical instruments such as the *cartonium*, talking machine, *manopan* and *calliston*.

187. *Poïkilorgue*, **Cavaillé-Coll and Son, Paris, c. 1834** (inv. M3140)

188. Harmonium, Alexandre-François Debain, Paris, c. 1867 (inv. 3586)

189. Soprano cecilium, A. Quentin de Gromard, France, c. 1861 (inv. M2406)

With the French harmonium of Alexandre-François Debain* (1842), we see the birth of a salon instrument with different characteristics, marking it off from the *orgue expressif*: a systematic division of the keyboard into two halves — bass and treble — each with its own registers.

Octave couplers reinforced the sound level, and the expression stop allowed the performer to vary directly the level of the sound. Especially with the work of the Mustel family, the harmonium was to become a real concert instrument, no longer limited to France, but also used in Germany and England. This evolution happened rather in the enlargement of the technical possibilities of the instrument without any modifications of its basic principles. The Parisian salon instrument opened the path to the construction of instruments of quality, such as the *Kunst-harmonium*. Cheap instruments were also made to replace the pipe organ; this is especially true of the *cottage organ* and the *American organ*.

Other experiments, just as original, mostly found themselves in a dead end. Even the popular harmonica, first perfected under the name of *harmoniphon*, was raised to the rank of a pseudo artistic instrument. The melophone and the cecilium* came from praiseworthy attempts at making a new instrument. The melophone came from the desire of the watchmaker Lerclerc (1837) to make an instrument in the form of a guitar with free reeds. The instrument displayed was made by A. Brown (Paris). The cecilium (1861), invented by A. Quentin de Gromard, came from the same reflection. It was a new expressive instrument, using free reeds, based on the quartet (soprano, alto, tenor and bass). The general form of the instrument and the playing technique were close to those of the violoncello. According to the inventor, the possibilities of this instrument knew no limits. It could be used as a solo instrument, as an accompanying instrument or even as a quartet.

82. Keys and keyboard instruments

Keys and keyboards are typical of the West. In some cases keys are used to action indirectly the vibrating part of an instrument. Examples include harpsichord plectra and piano hammers. Keys transform the muscular energy into mechanical energy and thus into sound.

Keys of an organ or harmonium have a completely different function: they open or close wind channels. They can be compared to the keys of wind instruments, used to change the pitch of the note.

Keys have also been used on other instruments than conventional keyboard instruments. In the late 19th century, the dentist Schaffner adapted a keyboard mechanism to the transverse flute, the oboe and the clarinet. In some cases, such as the monochord, the keys replace the function of the fingers in shortening the string length.

Faced with the passion for virtuosity at the beginning of the 19th century, teachers dreamt up a whole series of mechanical devices which would help budding virtuosi to achieve even greater finger agility. Once in use however, these devices were seen to be real instruments of torture. The dactylion, patented in 1836 by Herz, himself a pianist, teacher, composer and piano maker, enjoyed considerable success. Designed to loosen and strengthen the fingers, it was made up of two parallel wooden bars. The first was fixed to the front of the keyboard and was used to guide the hands. The second, placed parallel to the first, had ten rings, one for each finger, which were attached to springs that could be adjusted to give greater resistance.

The chirogymnast* was invented in 1840 by Casimir Martin. The model on display is made up of nine small devices, each intended for a specific exercise: extension of the hand span, the spreading of the fingers, the raising of the ring finger, increased thumb movement, increased strength of touch, equalisation of the touch, increased independence of each finger, and so on.

As for the ochydactyl*, this looks like a finger vice, and was intended to increase the suppleness of the fingers. It was invented by Georges Rétif between 1925 and 1930, which just goes to show that these devices were in use for many years. Nonetheless, many people were sceptical of the new inventions right from the start. François-Joseph Fétis, the first director of the Brussels Royal Music Conservatory, on presenting the dactylion to Frédéric Kalkbrenner, was heard to say: 'It seems to me that the dactylion is only good for catching mice'. 'No', replied Kalkbrenner, 'Monsieur Henri Herz made it for catching fools'.

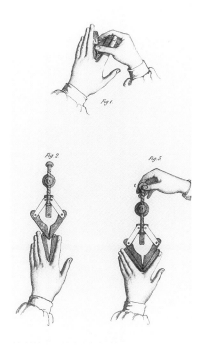

190. *Le chirogymnaste*, plates illustrating the
method of Casimir Martin, Paris, 1846.
© KBR, Brussels, Fétis 6293

191. Ochydactyl, Georges Rétif, Paris, c. 1925 (inv. 3559)

83. Bells and carillons

Bells are found in nearly all civilisations. They are made from different materials such as bronze, iron, pottery, crystal and even wood. The oldest bells were found in South-East Asia before they spread to China and the Middle East. Bells arrived in Europe via Asia minor and the Grecian and Roman civilisations. The Church gave them a Christian signification by consecrating them and integrating them into the cult. The bell called *signum*, either a hand bell or bells on a wheel, regulated monastic life, sounding the hours and announcing the offices. From the 6th century on, the large bell*, sounded by means of a rope, appeared in church towers. Monks, who were both foundry workers and experts, also developed new techniques. The large bells, initially made with the procedure known as 'lost wax casting', was cast from the 12th century on using a technique still in use in the 20th century.

192. Bell, Pieter Van den Gheyn, Mechelen, 1594 (inv. 70.002)

The Van den Gheyn family was one of the most remarkable dynasties of bell founders in the Southern Low Countries. They were active from 1529 to 1833. After, the bell foundry was taken over by the Aerschodt family until 1943, then by Sergeys until 1981.

Progressively, more and more heavy bells were suspended in the belfries of parish churches.

The developing towns brought new needs. Many new types of bell appeared alongside the hanging church bell: the calling bell, the tithing bell, the fire bell, the alert bell, the bell of triumph, the work bell, etc. Along with this development, the monk-casters were supplanted by itinerant casters. The communal life of the Middle Ages was governed by work, prayer and rest. Thus developed, in the 13th century, the *horologium*, a mechanical system allowing the division of the day into unities of time. By combining a clock with a few *cymbala* — small bells originally played with a small hammer and used to accompany church music as well as for musical instruction — makers in the Southern Low Countries made a drum which actioned a mechanical musical clock.

Carillons

All sorts of tunes could be played on the bells independently from the clock 'for the honour of God' (Dunkirk, 1478). But this 'great novelty' (ibid.) evolved into a large instrument 'where the ropes are pulled by sticks', (Antwerp, 1482). Thus the carillon* was invented, 'for the distraction of the inhabitants' (Bruges, 1546).

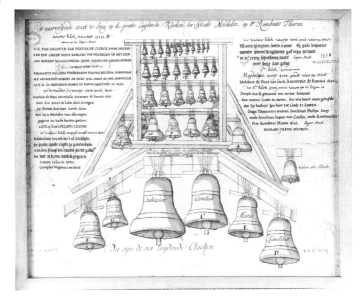

193. Plan and commentaries on a carillon and bells, Mechelen, end of the 17th century.
© Stedelijk Museum, Hof van Busleyden, Mechelen

84. Mechanical instruments

Mechanical instruments reproduce music which has previously been fixed on cylinders, disks, rolls of paper or books. They appeared a few centuries before our era before reaching a first peak in the Renaissance, then became all the rage at the end of the 19th and the beginning of the 20th centuries.

Mechanical instruments have seen an enormous range of applications, in popular circles as well as in the bourgeoisie. An incredible number of variants includes the carillon, the music box, the theatre organ, the pianola, the orchestrion, the mechanical piano* and the cartonium. Some instruments are known by the name of the manufacturer: the Limonaire, the Kalliston, the Wurlitzer, etc. Supplanted by modern instruments of reproduction like discs and magnetic tape, the mechanical instrument is now a collectors' item.

194. Mechanical piano *Antiphonel*, Alexandre-François Debain, Paris, c. 1860 (inv. 4180)

85. Mechanical instruments in salons

Mechanical musical instruments make sounds without the intervention of a performer, but their programme is predefined. Used in salons, ballrooms and even concert halls, they are typical of the end of the 19th and the beginning of the 20th centuries. Thanks to music boxes, clocks with flutes, serinettes, cylinder pianos, orchestrions and pneumatic systems placed before the keyboard, the bourgeois music lover could have access to the world of great music.

With the serinette, a sort of small organ operated by a handle and conceived to teach canaries new tunes, an attempt was already made to reproduce dance tunes mechanically. Its successors were to be much larger. About 1900, they were to be found in hotel halls, but also in popular establishments.

Mechanical spinet

The mechanical spinet, with dancing automatons in the upper part, was one of the first sorts of mechanical salon instruments. These dancers performed different forms of old dances according to the disc introduced.

195. Cylinder spinet, M. Le Conte, France, c. 1700 (inv. M1614)

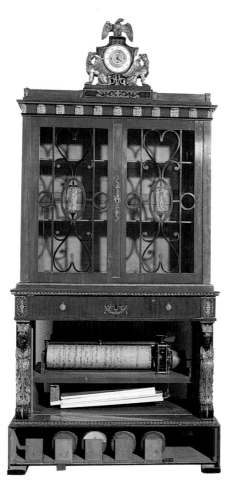

196. Showcase-desk with barrel organ, J.A. Hoyer, Vienna, c. 1815 (inv. M3144)

86. Popular mechanical instruments

Street corners and public places became the favoured domain of barrel organs and player pianos. Originally the barrel organ* was little more than a large bird organ (serinette) hung around the neck or placed on a stand. The largest models were placed on a barrow and they would be played at balls and village fairs, while the smaller street models were often replaced by the reed organ. The pianola or mechanical piano fell into the same social context. The large barrel organs were not only to be found on street corners, but also in dance halls and in open-air cafés. Like most mechanical instruments the music was initially put onto the cylinder. From about 1900 onwards the cylinder was gradually abandoned in favour of the organ book — a series of perforated cards, which were stuck together and had perforations cut into them to recreate the music.

197. Anonymous, *Beggar playing the barrel organ*, end of the 19th century. MIM, Brussels

87. The componium

The most important inventions of Diederich Nicolaus Winkel (Lippstadt, 1777 - Amsterdam, 1826) 'maker and installer of musical instruments and finely wrought mechanical instruments', were the metronome (1814) and the componium (1821).

In late 19th century orchestrions, there is a rotating cylinder which, in synchronisation with the piece being played, returns to its starting point at the same time as the end of the piece being played. The componium is a variant of the orchestrion incorporating an aleatoric mechanism actioned by one or two wooden cylinders which move both the keyboard and the registers of the instrument.

The componium includes two complementary synchronised cylinders, both working continuously. The music, in groups of two bars, is notated alternately on each of the two cylinders. While one is playing, the other is silent. During

198. Componium, Diederich Nicolaus Winkel, Amsterdam, 1821 (inv. M456)

the period of silence, the non-playing cylinder can move to another position, while the other cylinder plays its two bars. Inside the instrument, there is a programmer which, according to an aleatoric position of the inner mechanism, decides whether or not the cylinder will move to another unpredictable position. The componium cannot compose new music but can play for several million years without using up all of its possibilities for making variations.

The MIM has simulated a componium on computer, thanks to the sponsorship of Fortis AG.

199. An original componium case. Advertisement for a componium concert in London, 1830. MIM, Brussels

88. Electrical sound amplification

The amplification and reproduction of sound by means of an electrical transducer were developed only from 1924. This new technology was applied first to gramophones and then to recording devices. The first gramophones were purely mechanical. A contact microphone was first used on a guitar in 1928. A few years later, the violin was amplified with the same technique and the Hawaiian guitar, a sort of electric spinet, was invented. The electric guitar became extremely popular in the 1950s with the advent of the Rhythm & Blues pop music style. The electric guitar has since been made with a solid wooden body, but a 'semi-acoustical' guitar also exists, which has a hollow body.

200. Cylinder phonograph, Edison, USA, c. 1900 (inv. JT425)

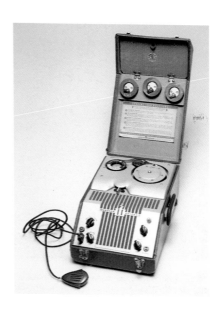

201. Wire recorder, Webster, Chicago, c. 1940 (inv. 99.020)

89. Electronic sound generation

Each new electronic instrument represents a phase in the development of sound generators towards the mastering of the acoustical spectrum. Before the First World War the differential sound between a fixed and a moveable frequency was often used. This is the technique used by the *Ondes Martenot* (1928) and by the *theremin* (1929). The *theremin* that we present is a copy of Big Briars. It does not use actual physical contact, but the proximity of the hand to the antennas. The left antenna determines the volume, the right the pitch.

Electronic music studios hardly appeared until after the Second World War. Herbert Eimert founded the prototype studio in Cologne in 1951. From the studio of the IPEM (Institute for Psycho-acoustics and Electronic Music) of the University of Ghent, we have many surviving instruments* which well illustrate this period: sine-wave generators, sound generators, ring modulators and a sequencer. The commercially produced synthesizers of the 1960s and 1970s made the techniques of electronic music easily available to a large public. The single channel *Korg M 20* works with the traditional sound waves of theoretical acoustics: sine waves, saw-tooth waves, square waves and impulsing. Already in 1930, the *Trautonium* used a saw-tooth wave generator and incandescent lights. The Wurlitzer electronic organ is an example of an instrument which uses twelve oscillators producing the twelve equal-tempered notes.

'The instruments which engineers must bring to perfection in collaboration with musicians will make all sounds available for use... We may say that such a rich diversity of timbres has heretofore been non-existent. The intensities are hardly variable. Thanks to the mechanical system we may indulge in endless dreams of both timbre and intensity' (Edgard Varèse, 1930).

202. Sequencers, cutting table, mixing table, sound filters and a bank of generators from the IPEM, Ghent, about 1970. MIM, Brussels

Photo credits

Atanassov, Vergilii (ill. 33)

Bayerisches Nationalmuseum München (ill. 133)

Bibliothèque nationale de France (ill. 92)

Boone, Hubert (ill. 34 & 43)

Bosmans, Wim (ill. 48)

Demeulenaere, Ritteke (ill. 24)

Dubois, Rémy (ill. 14)

Editions Mardaga; Jacky Collot (ill. 120, 136, 166, 173, 175 & 177)

Fondation Roi Baudouin/Koning Boudewijn Stichting, Brussels; Philippe de Formanoir (ill. 167)

Fürst Wallerstein Schlösser und Museen Harburg; Hirsch (ill. 111)

Helffer, Mireille (ill. 72)

IRPA/KIK, Brussels (ill. 13)

KBR, Brussels (ill. 18, 184 & 190)

Kunsthistorisches Museum Wien (ill. 7, 15 & 19)

Le Soir; J. Heylemans (ill. 10)

Leupen, Ingrid (ill. 75)

MIM, Brussels; Jean Boucher (ill. 1 & 2)

MIM, Brussels; Christian De Bruyne (ill. 9)

MIM, Brussels; Ferdinand-Joseph De Hen (ill. 61)

MIM, Brussels; Luc Schrobiltgen (excepted ill. 5, 12, 22, 76, 120, 136, 166, 167, 172, 173, 175 & 177)

MIM, Brussels; Johan Van Dijk (ill. 66)

MIM, Brussels; Philippe Van Steenseel (ill. 172)

MIM, Brussels; Geert Vermeiren (ill. 4)

MRAH/KMKG, Brussels; Raymond Mommaerts (ill. 5, 12, 22 & 76)

Münchner Stadtmuseum, Grafiksammlung (ill. 128)

Musée des Beaux-Arts, Nîmes (ill. 135)

Museo del Prado – Fotografia cedida e autorizada por el Patrimonio nacional, Madrid (ill. 79 & 80)

Museum für Geschichte der Stadt Leipzig (ill. 104)

National Gallery of Art, Washington DC. Board of Trustees, 1998 (ill. 148)

Royal College of Music, London, Department of Portraits (ill. 107)

Real Biblioteca de San Lorenzo, Escorial. Fotografia cedida e autorizada por el Patrimonio nacional, Madrid (ill. 77)

Stedelijk Museum 'Hof van Busleyden', Mechelen (ill. 193)

Szabó, Tibor (ill. 38)

Van der Ven, D.J. (ill. 32)

Veulemans, Dirk (ill. 45)

Worcester Art Museum, Worcester, Massachussetts, Museum purchase (ill. 131)

Sponsors of the MIM
in order of the importance of their contribution
(the list is correct up to the publication date of the *Visitor's Guide*, 15th March 2000)

FORTIS AG
Restoration of nine instruments; copies of seven old instruments; video equipment; six concerts and six CDs

NATIONAL LOTTERY
The sound system in the exhibition rooms; equipment of the 'Espace Son'; video equipment for the concert hall

EUROPEAN COMMISSION
Directorate General for education and culture
Systems for the 'Espace Son'

CEMENTERIES CBR
Development of the restaurant in the Art Nouveau style in the Saintenoy building

AGF-BELGIUM / ALLIANZ GROUP
Concerts, prestigious booklets and the CD of the inauguration

CITIBANK
Computer system and computerisation of the library

ETEX GROUP
Acquisitions for the collection

AXA ROYALE BELGE
CD discovery of music; workshop for the handicapped

SPADEL
Development and equipment for the restaurant terrace

3M
Illustrations and directions for the rooms; Internet site

BRUXELLES / BRUSSEL 2000
Inauguration concert and concerts of September, 2000

KBC BANK & VERZEKERING / CBC BANQUE & ASSURANCE
Publication of the Visitor's Guide and the six Guides of the Collections

JP MORGAN
Sculptures in the reception hall

PIERRE MARDAGA, éditeur
Help with the publications

ROI BAUDOUIN FOUNDATION
Experiments in the Garden of Orpheus

HENRY FORD FUNDS
Restoration of a grand piano

GEAC
Computer programme for the cataloguing of the library

MICROSOFT
Computer programmes

RTBF-MUSIQUE 3
Recording the orchestra for the inaugural CD

THE FRIENDS OF THE MIM
Audio equipment for the Garden of Orpheus for the hard of hearing; restoration of a harp

GLAVERBEL
Support for the showcases

Practical informations

Musical Instruments Museum (MIM)
IVth department of the Royal Museums of Art and History
Rue Montagne de la Cour, 2 - B-1000 Bruxelles

- Opening hours: Tuesday, Wednesday, Friday: 9 h 30 to 17 h / Thursday: 9 h 30 to 20 h /
  Saturday and Sunday: 10 h to 17 h
- Closed on 1 January, 1 May, 1 et 11 November, 25 December
- Entrance fee: adults: 150 BEF (3,72 €) / children (6-12 ans): 50 BEF (1,24 €) /
  reductions: 100 BEF (2,48 €)
- Free access to the shops and the restaurants
- Guided visits on request
- Informations et reservations: tel.: 02/545.01.30 - 02/545.01.53 (Education Department) /
  fax: 02/545.01.78 / e-mail: info@mim.fgov.be / http://www.mim.fgov.be
- Access:
  Metro: Parc or Gare centrale
  Train: Gare centrale
  Bus: 20, 38, 60, 71, 95, 96 (bus stop Royale)
  Car park (paying): Congrès-Albertine

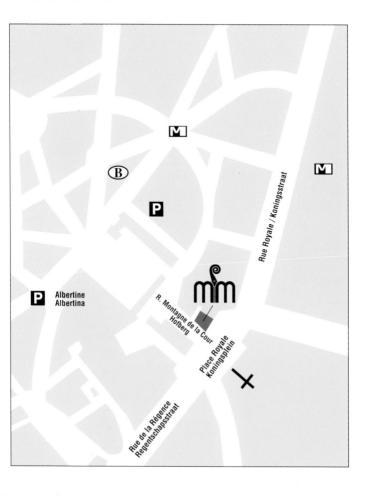

Imprimé en Belgique par Pierre Mardaga, Liège.